MW01687460

Become an Officer in
Law Enforcement
Getting the Edge

by
Robert J. Piel
Paul van der Linden

Career Publishing Inc.
Orange, CA

Senior Editor and Project Coordinator: Marilyn M. Martin
Illustrator: Alan J. Borie
Additional Graphics obtained from the LifeART™ collections from Techpool Studios Inc, Cleveland , OH
Cover Photo Credits
Upper Left: Long Beach, CA Police Department
Lower Left: Los Angeles, CA Police Department
Upper Right, Center, and Lower Left: Robert J. Piel

This guide was produced by Desktop Publishing techniques using Microsoft Word, Adobe PageMaker, MacroMedia FreeHand, and Adobe PhotoShop on Macintosh computers and output to a LaserMaster Unity 1800XL-O printer

ISBN 0-89262-495-7
Library of Congress Catalog Card Number 95-071150

PRINTED AND BOUND IN THE UNITED STATES OF AMERICA

Career
PUBLISHING INCORPORATED
VOCATIONAL & APPLIED TECHNOLOGY
910 N. Main St.,
P.O. Box 5486
Orange, CA 92667

National/Canada
1 (800) 854-4014
Includes Alaska, Hawaii and Puerto Rico

FAX 1-714-532-0180

10 9 8 7 6 5 4 3 2 1

Contents

Acknowledgments

I would like to thank my wife, Jacqueline, and my three daughters, Nichole, Natalie, and Christina. All of whom helped with the creation of this book.

I am dedicating this book to my chosen profession, Law Enforcement, the most fascinating and challenging career that anyone can experience. And finally, to my fellow officers with the Montebello Police Department and the Latah County Sheriff's Office.

Thank You.
Robert J. Piel

I would like to thank my wife, Lori, for the loving support, caring, and encouragement only a police officer's wife would know; my parents for their support and the values they installed in me; a special thanks to E.J. "Lucky" Plantico for his guidance during my younger years; and last but not least, my stepson Brandon, and his daily question, "Did ya get a bad guy today?"

Thank You.
Paul van der Linden

We both would also like to thank our publisher, Harold Haase, for his faith in our book; our editor, Marilyn Martin, for overseeing its production; and our graphics artist, Alan Borie, for turning our words into art.

About the Authors

After moving to Idaho from the Los Angeles area, Robert J. Piel and Paul van der Linden began their collaboration as authors on ***Become an Officer in Law Enforcement: Getting the Edge.*** When Detective Piel approached Officer van der Linden with his idea of writing a book to help others obtain a position in law enforcement, it was with the idea that double the training and experience would produce a more useful and accurate book. van der Linden heartily agreed, and this guidebook was written.

Robert J. Piel is currently a Police Officer in the newly incorporated city of Federal Way, Washington. Born in Pomona, California, Detective Piel began his career in law enforcement with the Montebello, California Police Department in 1983. Montebello is an East Los Angeles suburb, and he was assigned to the Patrol Division, Anti-Gang Unit and Background Investigation for new recruits.

Following his graduation from the National Academy of Lie Detection, he became a certified Polygraph Examiner. In addition to his duties with the Montebello Police Department, he worked on a part-time basis with K&K Lie Detection, which specializes in commercial business security and contracted-service with several police agencies for specific-issue and pre-employment testing.

After moving his family to Moscow, Idaho, a university town of 18,000 residents and 10,000 students, in 1990, Piel tested and was selected as a Presentence Investigator for the State of Idaho Parole and Probation Department.

During the time he and van der Linden were researching and writing this book, Piel accepted a position with the Latah County Sheriff's Office as a deputy sheriff. He later worked with the Sheriff's Office as a Detective.

A native of Covina, California, **Paul C. van der Linden's** interest in becoming an officer in law enforcement began in high school when he was a member of the Police Explorers for four years. He holds a number of certificates in achievement, physical fitness, and participation from various youth-related law enforcement activities. Following his graduation from high school, he worked in several capacities in the security field.

van der Linden has over fifteen years of experience in Law Enforcement ranging from dispatching, background investigations, and patrol to the Detective Bureau and homicide investigations.

In 1982, van der Linden became a Reserve Police Officer for the City of Irwindale, California. He then became a full-time Police Officer for Irwindale where he served for nine years. He was retired medically following a disability that occurred while on the job.

Now residing in Northern Idaho with his family, he operates his own Carpet Sculpting business and serves as a volunteer in the Sheriff's Department to assist when needed.

Preface

In the field of law enforcement, there are literally thousands upon thousands of positions nationwide waiting for qualified applicants. ***Become an Officer in Law Enforcement: Getting the Edge*** is a comprehensive manual designed to walk the law enforcement applicant through each stage of what can often be a grueling and disappointing hiring process. You will find this guidebook thoroughly explains each phase of process. It is not limited to only the written examination.

Law Enforcement is an ever-expanding field that must grow with the population. From the F.B.I. and the Secret Service to all local police and sheriff agencies, the opportunities are unlimited. The only thing that may stand between you and a high-paying career is how you rate against your competition.

The difference between success and failure may depend on your having **the edge**. Our manual will walk you through the potential obstacles you are likely to encounter as you prepare for one of the most fascinating careers known – that of Law Enforcement.

Become an Officer in Law Enforcement: Getting the Edge was developed by interviewing experienced police officers, polygraph examiners, background investigators, and psychologists. The information was carefully drafted to meet the criteria of most federal, state, and local law enforcement agencies. As you read this book, we are confident it will prepare you to surpass the average applicant and advance toward the career of your dreams.

The following page lists several agencies that require the completion of a hiring procedure similar, if not identical, to the process described in this handbook. It is also a reference guide that you can use to consider which area of law enforcement you wish to enter.

Remember, the field is enormous and the opportunities are unlimited. Take the time to properly prepare, and you will achieve your goals.

Good Luck!

Reference List

Alcohol Beverage Control (State & Federal)
Airport Police (Private)
Alcohol Tobacco and Firearms (Federal)
Armored Truck Guards (Private)
City Municipal Police Agencies (State)
Central Intelligence Agency (Federal)
College and University Campus Police (State & Private)
County Park Patrol & Park Rangers (County & Federal)
County, State, and Federal Marshals
Drug Enforcement Agency (Federal)
Department of Corrections (State & Federal officers)
Department of Defense Police (Federal)
Department of Energy Police (Federal)
Department of Immigration & Naturalization (Federal)
Department of Motor Vehicles Fraud & Theft Investigators (State)
District Attorney Investigator (City & State)
F.A.A. Investigators (Federal)
Federal Bureau of Investigation (Federal)
Federal Postal Police & Inspectors (Federal)
Fish & Game Wardens (State & Federal)
Housing Authority (State & City)
Indian Reservation Police (Federal)
Library of Congress Police (Federal)
Military Police Criminal Investigation Division (Federal)
National Security Agency (Federal)
Parole and Probation (State & Federal)
Public School Police (City)
Railroad Police (Private)
Safety Police (City & State)
Secret Service (Federal)
Subway Police (Larger Metropolitan Areas)
Transit Police (City)
United States Capitol Police (Federal)
United States Congress Police (Federal)
United States Customs (Federal)
United States Border Patrol (Federal)
United States Mint Police (Federal)
Welfare Fraud Investigators (State & Federal)

Chapter One
The Application

Objectives

When you have completed this chapter, you will understand how to:

1. Pick a work location
2. Obtain applications from agencies
3. Complete applications
4. Return applications to the agencies

Key Terms

- application
- oral interview
- background investigation

Introduction

You have decided to become a law enforcement officer. Now you are wondering what is the best way to obtain employment with one of the agencies. There are four simple steps to follow at the beginning of your search.

- Decide where you want to work
- Pick up applications
- Fill out applications
- Return them to the agencies

Deciding Where You Want to Work

Before you can apply for employment, you must decide where you would like to work. Often the best way is to list the locations you think are ideal places to live and work. Then make a list of all of the positive features of each area and a list of all of the negative features. Measure them against one another to determine which area may best suit your needs.

Figure 1-1: *Choosing a place to work*

Many people find the Chamber of Commerce a helpful tool. They are usually willing to send general information about an area and existing opportunities. A visit to the different locations will often assist you in making a choice. After you have obtained as much information as you think you need, study it and make your decision. The next step then is to gather **applications** from the law enforcement agencies in the area.

application: a form to be completed by a person seeking employment

We recommend that you apply to several different agencies as a safeguard. The agency or area you like best may not have an opening, or another applicant may be chosen for the position. Always have a backup plan.

Some agencies will mail an application to you upon request; however, it is usually better to apply in person. An example of such a successful strategy is a Police officer from southern California who plotted a course on a map that included the agencies and the areas in which he would like to work. He then spent the necessary time to drive to each of the agencies and gather applications.

This may sound like a radical method, but it worked for him. The time and effort were well spent. He received several job offers and is now a homicide detective for a large police department.

Picking Up the Application

When you pick up the applications, be polite and dress professionally. A man is usually better received if he is wearing a suit and tie. A woman should dress in a suit or very tailored outfit. Although others may be able to help you, ask to speak with the person in charge of recruiting. Ask questions about positions that are open or they anticipate will be open in the future. Remember, these are busy people. Their time is important, so try to be brief when you make your inquiries.

When you pick up your application, you also are often given a full list of cities in the state. You can then mark the form and indicate those areas in which you would be willing to accept employment.

Figure 1-2: *Try to make a good impression*

When the conversation is over, thank them for their time. Remember, first impressions do count. Whether they give serious consideration to your completed application may depend on how good an impression you made upon them when you picked it up.

Completing the Application

Take your time to complete the application. The application must be neat and concise. Everything must be easily readable. If at all possible, use a typewriter. You may even wish to make a copy of the application, complete it, and then copy the information onto the original application. This procedure may help you to avoid making mistakes and then having to correct them.

If a typewriter is not available, use a pen with black ink. Black ink looks professional and reproduces on photocopiers better. Remember, all questions on the application must be answered. Names, dates, and addresses must be accurate. Verify all of the information before you enter it. If you are unsure of the meaning of any of the questions on the application, take the time to find out exactly what information is needed.

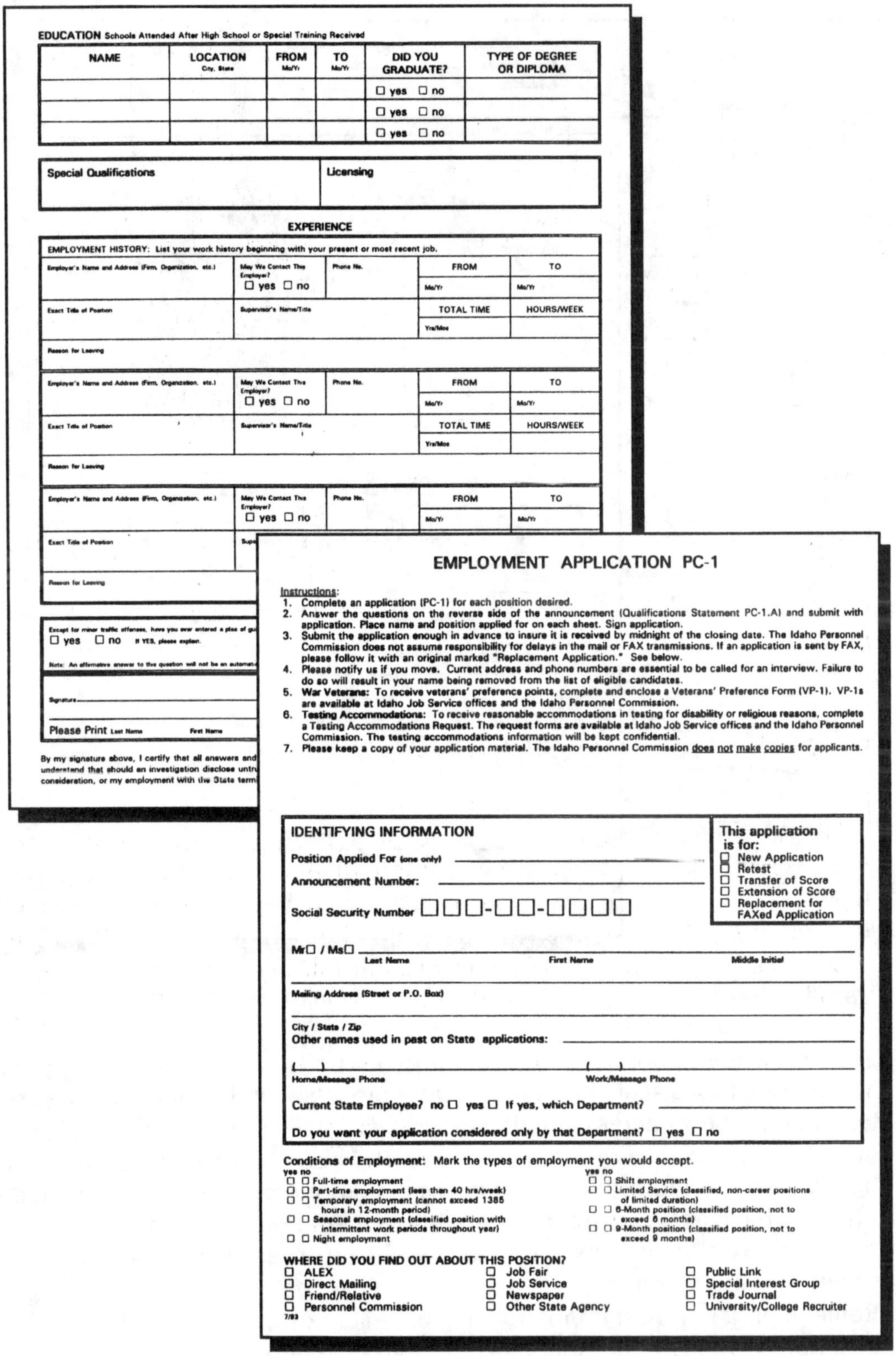

EDUCATION Schools Attended After High School or Special Training Received

NAME	LOCATION City, State	FROM Mo/Yr	TO Mo/Yr	DID YOU GRADUATE?	TYPE OF DEGREE OR DIPLOMA
				☐ yes ☐ no	
				☐ yes ☐ no	
				☐ yes ☐ no	

Special Qualifications | Licensing

EXPERIENCE

EMPLOYMENT HISTORY: List your work history beginning with your present or most recent job.

Employer's Name and Address (Firm, Organization, etc.)	May We Contact This Employer? ☐ yes ☐ no	Phone No.	FROM Mo/Yr	TO Mo/Yr
Exact Title of Position	Supervisor's Name/Title		TOTAL TIME Yrs/Mos	HOURS/WEEK
Reason for Leaving				
Employer's Name and Address (Firm, Organization, etc.)	May We Contact This Employer? ☐ yes ☐ no	Phone No.	FROM Mo/Yr	TO Mo/Yr
Exact Title of Position	Supervisor's Name/Title		TOTAL TIME Yrs/Mos	HOURS/WEEK
Reason for Leaving				
Employer's Name and Address (Firm, Organization, etc.)	May We Contact This Employer? ☐ yes ☐ no	Phone No.	FROM Mo/Yr	TO Mo/Yr
Exact Title of Position				
Reason for Leaving				

Except for minor traffic offenses, have you ever entered a plea of gu... ☐ yes ☐ no If YES, please explain.

Note: An affirmative answer to this question will not be an automati...

Signature

Please Print Last Name First Name

By my signature above, I certify that all answers and ... understand that should an investigation disclose untru... consideration, or my employment with the State term...

EMPLOYMENT APPLICATION PC-1

Instructions:
1. Complete an application (PC-1) for each position desired.
2. Answer the questions on the reverse side of the announcement (Qualifications Statement PC-1.A) and submit with application. Place name and position applied for on each sheet. Sign application.
3. Submit the application enough in advance to insure it is received by midnight of the closing date. The Idaho Personnel Commission does not assume responsibility for delays in the mail or FAX transmissions. If an application is sent by FAX, please follow it with an original marked "Replacement Application." See below.
4. Please notify us if you move. Current address and phone numbers are essential to be called for an interview. Failure to do so will result in your name being removed from the list of eligible candidates.
5. War Veterans: To receive veterans' preference points, complete and enclose a Veterans' Preference Form (VP-1). VP-1s are available at Idaho Job Service offices and the Idaho Personnel Commission.
6. Testing Accommodations: To receive reasonable accommodations in testing for disability or religious reasons, complete a Testing Accommodations Request. The request forms are available at Idaho Job Service offices and the Idaho Personnel Commission. The testing accommodations information will be kept confidential.
7. Please keep a copy of your application material. The Idaho Personnel Commission does not make copies for applicants.

IDENTIFYING INFORMATION

Position Applied For (one only) ____

Announcement Number: ____

Social Security Number ☐☐☐-☐☐-☐☐☐☐

This application is for:
☐ New Application
☐ Retest
☐ Transfer of Score
☐ Extension of Score
☐ Replacement for FAXed Application

Mr☐ / Ms☐ ____ Last Name First Name Middle Initial

Mailing Address (Street or P.O. Box)

City / State / Zip

Other names used in past on State applications: ____

( ) Home/Message Phone ( ) Work/Message Phone

Current State Employee? no ☐ yes ☐ If yes, which Department? ____

Do you want your application considered only by that Department? ☐ yes ☐ no

Conditions of Employment: Mark the types of employment you would accept.

yes no
☐ ☐ Full-time employment
☐ ☐ Part-time employment (less than 40 hrs/week)
☐ ☐ Temporary employment (cannot exceed 1385 hours in 12-month period)
☐ ☐ Seasonal employment (classified position with intermittent work periods throughout year)
☐ ☐ Night employment

yes no
☐ ☐ Shift employment
☐ ☐ Limited Service (classified, non-career positions of limited duration)
☐ ☐ 6-Month position (classified position, not to exceed 6 months)
☐ ☐ 9-Month position (classified position, not to exceed 9 months)

WHERE DID YOU FIND OUT ABOUT THIS POSITION?
☐ ALEX
☐ Direct Mailing
☐ Friend/Relative
☐ Personnel Commission
☐ Job Fair
☐ Job Service
☐ Newspaper
☐ Other State Agency
☐ Public Link
☐ Special Interest Group
☐ Trade Journal
☐ University/College Recruiter

7/93

Figure 1-3: *Sample Application*

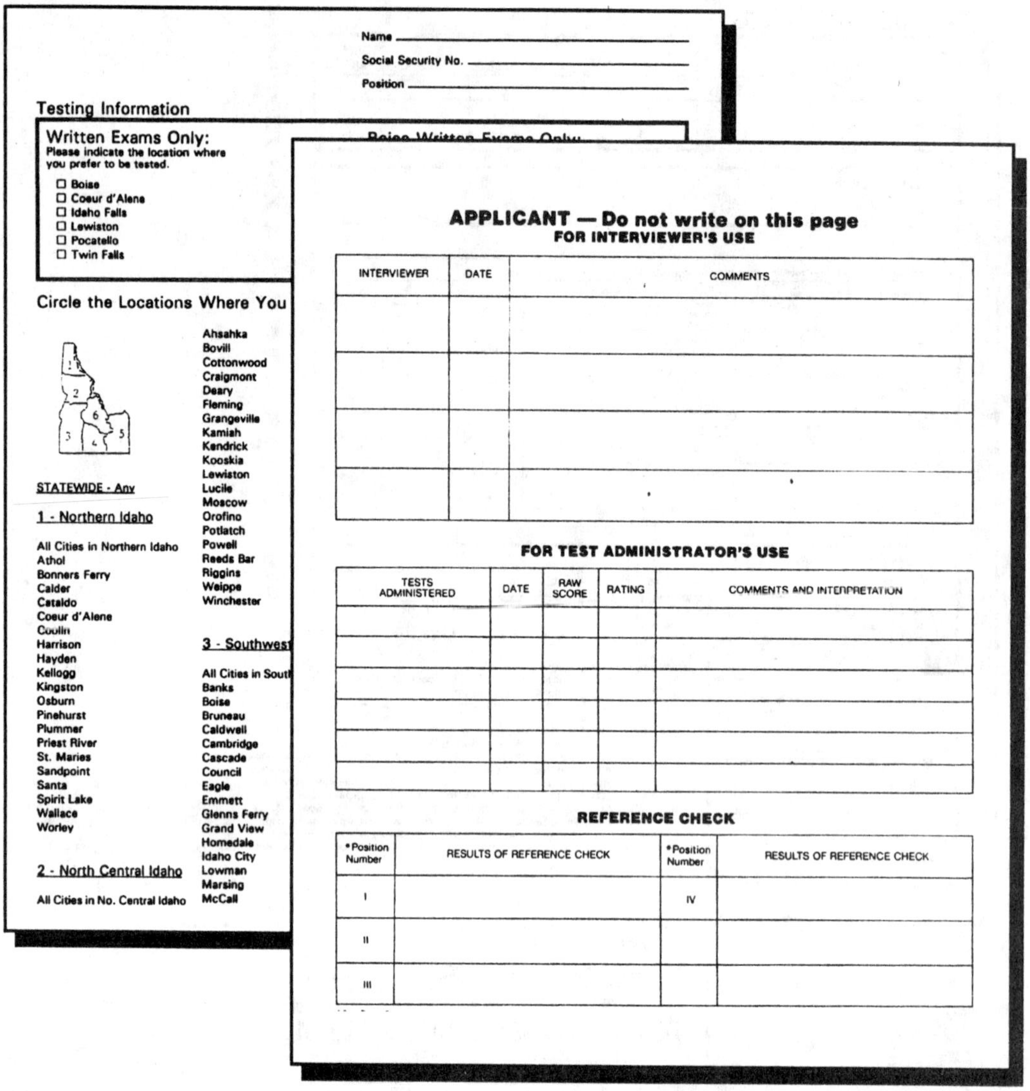

Name
Social Security No.
Position

Testing Information

Written Exams Only:
Please indicate the location where you prefer to be tested.
- ☐ Boise
- ☐ Coeur d'Alene
- ☐ Idaho Falls
- ☐ Lewiston
- ☐ Pocatello
- ☐ Twin Falls

Circle the Locations Where You

STATEWIDE - Any

1 - Northern Idaho

All Cities in Northern Idaho
Athol
Bonners Ferry
Calder
Cataldo
Coeur d'Alene
Coolin
Harrison
Hayden
Kellogg
Kingston
Osburn
Pinehurst
Plummer
Priest River
St. Maries
Sandpoint
Santa
Spirit Lake
Wallace
Worley

2 - North Central Idaho

All Cities in No. Central Idaho
Ahsahka
Bovill
Cottonwood
Craigmont
Deary
Fleming
Grangeville
Kamiah
Kendrick
Kooskia
Lewiston
Lucile
Moscow
Orofino
Potlatch
Powell
Reeds Bar
Riggins
Weippe
Winchester

3 - Southwest

All Cities in Sout
Banks
Boise
Bruneau
Caldwell
Cambridge
Cascade
Council
Eagle
Emmett
Glenns Ferry
Grand View
Homedale
Idaho City
Lowman
Marsing
McCall

APPLICANT — Do not write on this page
FOR INTERVIEWER'S USE

INTERVIEWER	DATE	COMMENTS

FOR TEST ADMINISTRATOR'S USE

TESTS ADMINISTERED	DATE	RAW SCORE	RATING	COMMENTS AND INTERPRETATION

REFERENCE CHECK

*Position Number	RESULTS OF REFERENCE CHECK	*Position Number	RESULTS OF REFERENCE CHECK
I		IV	
II			
III			

Figure 1-4: *Choice of location form from the State of Idaho and evaluation page*

Most applications also have a page that is reserved for the interviewer's and tester's comments and evaluations.

If necessary, call former employers and ask about employment dates to be sure you have accurate information. If you were released from an employment, briefly explain why. The reason will be revealed later in the background investigation, so it is always better to be truthful from the start. Remember, it is almost impossible to conceal information, so honesty is the best policy. Many departments will not give an applicant for employment further consideration if they discover dishonesty or evasion in the application process.

Figure 1-5: *Calling a former employer to verify employment dates*

Another important thing to understand is that the information you include or exclude will be used during your **oral interview** and **background investigation**. Hundreds of applicants are washed out of the hiring process for trying to withhold minor or otherwise non-disqualifing information.

oral interview: a formal meeting between an employer and a prospective employee to discuss a position and the applicant's qualifications

background investigation: a check by the potential employer of information given on the application and to determine if facts were withheld

Please understand this process is not designed to keep people out of the field. It is simply designed to screen out less qualified applicants. Law enforcement personnel must demonstrate integrity in all areas. When you try to hide any type of negative information from the background investigators, they consider it a challenge to find it and thus eliminate you from the testing.

Tell the truth at all times, and be prepared to answer any questions about your past. In some respects, this background check is similar to a security clearance for defense purposes. We will discuss problem backgrounds and how to present them in some of the following chapters.

When you have completed your application, proofread it. Then, if possible, have someone else check it for spelling errors. There is nothing worse than making it to an oral board interview only to have the interviewers quiz you about your misspelled words. Don't laugh. It really happens, especially with the smaller agencies.

An application that is completed correctly will resemble the one shown below and on the following page.

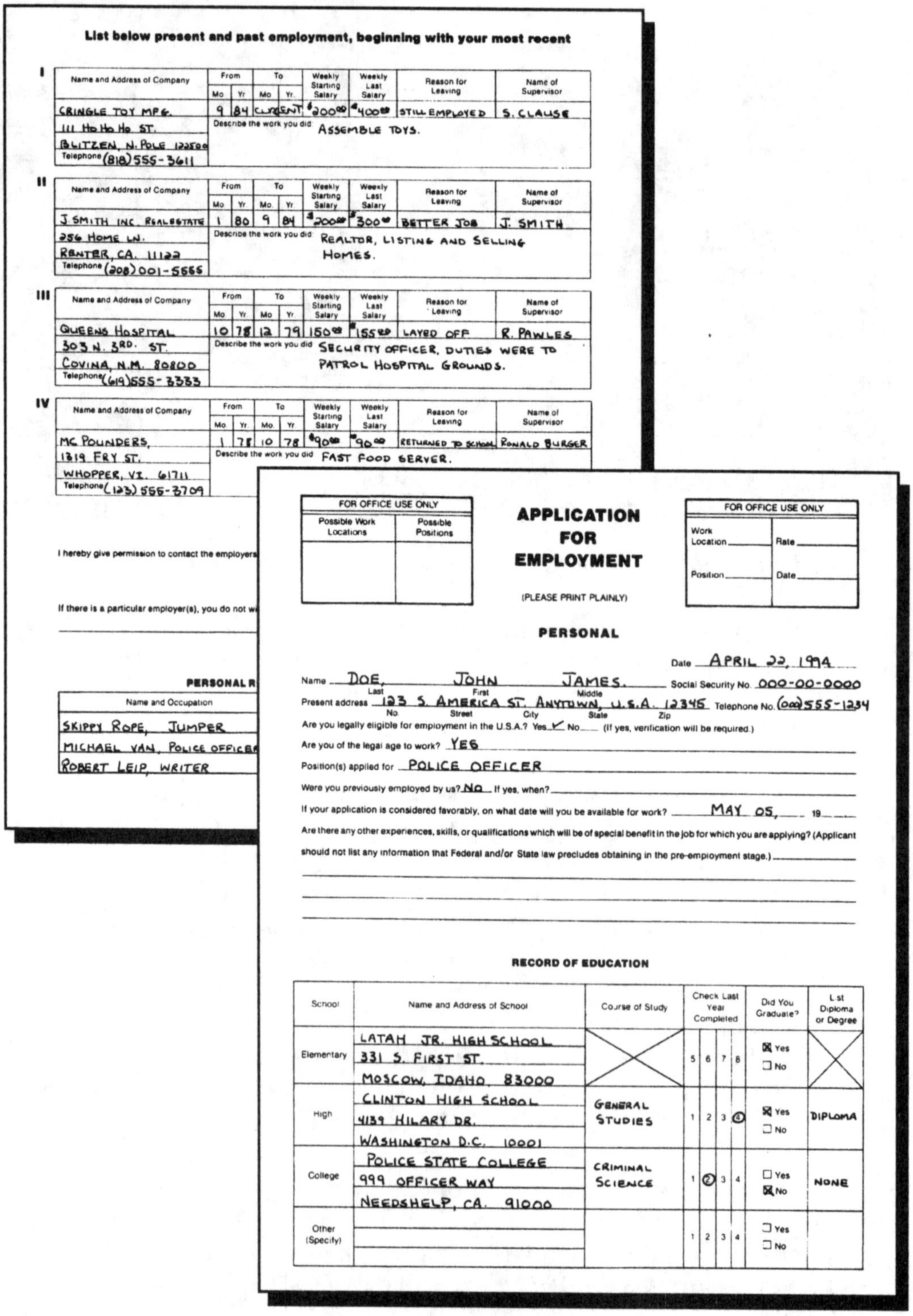

List below present and past employment, beginning with your most recent

	Name and Address of Company	From Mo	From Yr	To Mo	To Yr	Weekly Starting Salary	Weekly Last Salary	Reason for Leaving	Name of Supervisor
I	CRINGLE TOY MFG.	9	84	CURRENT		$200.00	$400.00	STILL EMPLOYED	S. CLAUSE
	111 HO HO HO ST.	Describe the work you did: ASSEMBLE TOYS.							
	BLITZEN, N. POLE 12250								
	Telephone (818) 555-3611								
II	J. SMITH INC. REALESTATE	1	80	9	84	$200.00	$300.00	BETTER JOB	J. SMITH
	256 HOME LN.	Describe the work you did: REALTOR, LISTING AND SELLING HOMES.							
	RENTER, CA. 11122								
	Telephone (208) 001-5555								
III	QUEENS HOSPITAL	10	78	12	79	150.00	$155.00	LAYED OFF	R. PAWLES
	303 N. 3RD. ST.	Describe the work you did: SECURITY OFFICER, DUTIES WERE TO PATROL HOSPITAL GROUNDS.							
	COVINA, N.M. 80800								
	Telephone (619) 555-3333								
IV	MC POUNDERS,	1	78	10	78	$90.00	$90.00	RETURNED TO SCHOOL	RONALD BURGER
	1319 FRY ST.	Describe the work you did: FAST FOOD SERVER.							
	WHOPPER, VT. 61711								
	Telephone (123) 555-3709								

I hereby give permission to contact the employers

If there is a particular employer(s), you do not w

PERSONAL R

Name and Occupation
SKIPPY ROPE, JUMPER
MICHAEL VAN, POLICE OFFICER
ROBERT LEIP, WRITER

FOR OFFICE USE ONLY	
Possible Work Locations	Possible Positions

APPLICATION FOR EMPLOYMENT

(PLEASE PRINT PLAINLY)

FOR OFFICE USE ONLY	
Work Location	Rate
Position	Date

PERSONAL

Date APRIL 22, 1994

Name DOE, JOHN JAMES. (Last, First, Middle) Social Security No. 000-00-0000

Present address 123 S. AMERICA ST. ANYTOWN, U.S.A. 12345 (No, Street, City, State, Zip) Telephone No. (000) 555-1234

Are you legally eligible for employment in the U.S.A.? Yes ✓ No ___ (If yes, verification will be required.)

Are you of the legal age to work? YES

Position(s) applied for POLICE OFFICER

Were you previously employed by us? NO If yes, when? ___

If your application is considered favorably, on what date will you be available for work? MAY 05, 19__

Are there any other experiences, skills, or qualifications which will be of special benefit in the job for which you are applying? (Applicant should not list any information that Federal and/or State law precludes obtaining in the pre-employment stage.)

RECORD OF EDUCATION

School	Name and Address of School	Course of Study	Check Last Year Completed	Did You Graduate?	List Diploma or Degree
Elementary	LATAH JR. HIGH SCHOOL, 331 S. FIRST ST., MOSCOW, IDAHO 83000		5 6 7 8	☒ Yes ☐ No	
High	CLINTON HIGH SCHOOL, 4139 HILARY DR., WASHINGTON D.C. 10001	GENERAL STUDIES	1 2 3 (4)	☒ Yes ☐ No	DIPLOMA
College	POLICE STATE COLLEGE, 999 OFFICER WAY, NEEDSHELP, CA. 91000	CRIMINAL SCIENCE	1 (2) 3 4	☐ Yes ☒ No	NONE
Other (Specify)			1 2 3 4	☐ Yes ☐ No	

***Figure 1-6a:** Completed application (Part 1)*

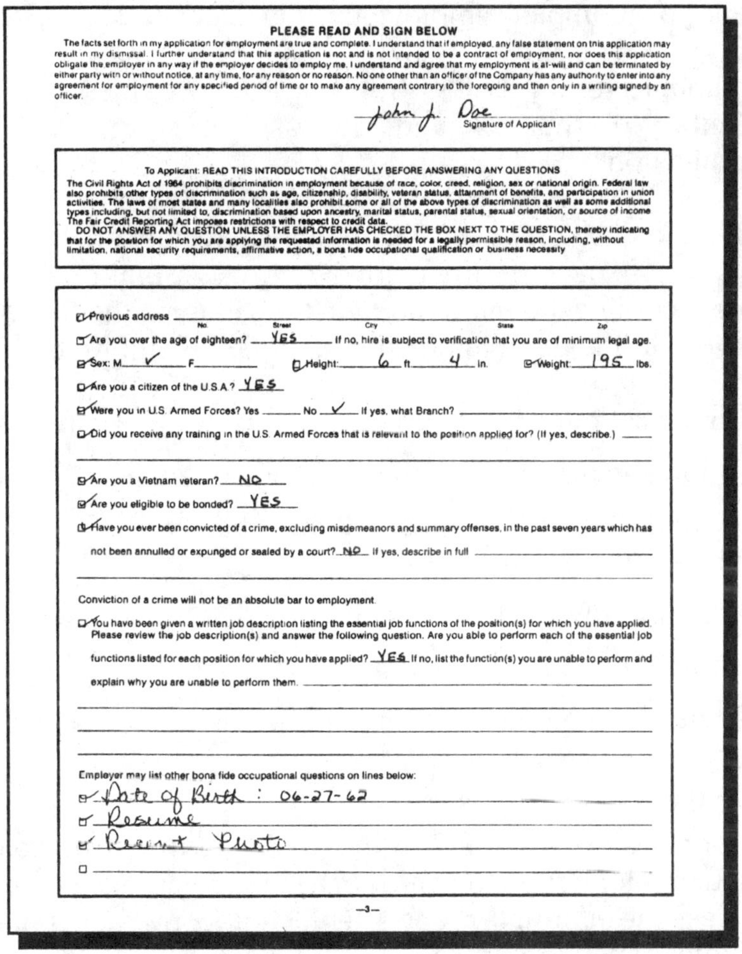

PLEASE READ AND SIGN BELOW

The facts set forth in my application for employment are true and complete. I understand that if employed, any false statement on this application may result in my dismissal. I further understand that this application is not and is not intended to be a contract of employment, nor does this application obligate the employer in any way if the employer decides to employ me. I understand and agree that my employment is at-will and can be terminated by either party with or without notice, at any time, for any reason or no reason. No one other than an officer of the Company has any authority to enter into any agreement for employment for any specified period of time or to make any agreement contrary to the foregoing and then only in a writing signed by an officer.

John J. Doe
Signature of Applicant

To Applicant: READ THIS INTRODUCTION CAREFULLY BEFORE ANSWERING ANY QUESTIONS

The Civil Rights Act of 1964 prohibits discrimination in employment because of race, color, creed, religion, sex or national origin. Federal law also prohibits other types of discrimination such as age, citizenship, disability, veteran status, attainment of benefits, and participation in union activities. The laws of most states and many localities also prohibit some or all of the above types of discrimination as well as some additional types including, but not limited to, discrimination based upon ancestry, marital status, parental status, sexual orientation, or source of income The Fair Credit Reporting Act imposes restrictions with respect to credit data.

DO NOT ANSWER ANY QUESTION UNLESS THE EMPLOYER HAS CHECKED THE BOX NEXT TO THE QUESTION, thereby indicating that for the position for which you are applying the requested information is needed for a legally permissible reason, including, without limitation, national security requirements, affirmative action, a bona fide occupational qualification or business necessity

☐ Previous address ______ (No. Street City State Zip)

☑ Are you over the age of eighteen? YES If no, hire is subject to verification that you are of minimum legal age.

☑ Sex: M ✓ F ______ ☑ Height: 6 ft. 4 in. ☑ Weight: 195 lbs.

☑ Are you a citizen of the U.S.A.? YES

☑ Were you in U.S. Armed Forces? Yes ______ No ✓ If yes, what Branch? ______

☑ Did you receive any training in the U.S. Armed Forces that is relevant to the position applied for? (If yes, describe.) ______

☑ Are you a Vietnam veteran? NO

☑ Are you eligible to be bonded? YES

☑ Have you ever been convicted of a crime, excluding misdemeanors and summary offenses, in the past seven years which has not been annulled or expunged or sealed by a court? NO If yes, describe in full ______

Conviction of a crime will not be an absolute bar to employment.

☑ You have been given a written job description listing the essential job functions of the position(s) for which you have applied. Please review the job description(s) and answer the following question. Are you able to perform each of the essential job functions listed for each position for which you have applied? YES If no, list the function(s) you are unable to perform and explain why you are unable to perform them. ______

Employer may list other bona fide occupational questions on lines below:

☑ Date of Birth: 06-27-62

☑ Resume

☑ Recent Photo

☐ ______

—3—

Figure 1-7: *Completed application (Part 2)*

Make a photocopy of your application when it is complete. You will need this copy when you move on to your oral board interview and background investigation. It will also come in handy if you are applying to several agencies at the same time.

The Resume

Because some agencies have different requirements associated with completing the application, we suggest you be prepared to submit a resume complete with employment history.

If the hiring agency requests a resume, we recommend a format similar to the resume shown on the opposite page be used as a guideline. This resume can be prepared on a typewriter and should not take a lot of time. Remember to include your complete employment and education history on the resume.

Do not submit a resume unless the hiring agency requests one. If you are not sure whether you should include one, ask the recruiter before you submit your application.

If you are asked to complete an employment history on the application and you run out of space on the application, use a plain piece of paper and continue recording the information in the same manner as you were on the application. Just keep in mind the following helpful hints.

- Do not submit any information that is **not** requested.
- Follow the instructions given on the application.
- If you have any questions, ask them before you submit the completed application.
- Do not falsify any information.
- Do not omit any information.
- Remember your application will be carefully *reviewed* and *verified* by the background investigator.

Any information you supply on the application will be compared to the background information they may have you complete a month or so in the future. Keep the information consistent. Photocopy your application, so you can refer to it later. In this way, you will not have to explain why there are differences in the information you gave to the agency.

The resume shown on the following page illustrates the type of resume you can submit if one is requested.

Jacqueline Lopez
1166 Bellbrook
Covina, CA 94555
(555) 555-1212

OBJECTIVE	To begin a life-long career in Law enforcement. I would like to promote through different assignments and become a knowledgeable and productive officer.
PROFESSIONAL EXPERIENCE	
10-90 to present	Real Estate Sales Century 22 Realty, Inc. 1134 W. San Bernard Rd. South Covina, CA 991722 List and sell real property, negotiate sales, advertise and promote properties for sales, promote my services, customer service to clients, schedule appointments and showings, pre-qualify buyers, market analysis, show property and keep clients informed of progress.
6-22-89/10-01-90	Pharmacy Technician Pharmacy Pay n' Save Drug Store 121 W. Hammel St. Covina, CA 91211 Assist Pharmacist with daily duties.
EDUCATION	
9-13-89 to present	Redview College Redview, CA 93645 Major: Administration of Justice Minor: English GPA: 3.0 College attended on a part-time basis since high school graduation. Degree anticipated within one year.
10-01-94	Real Estate License Obtained Longday Real Estate School Montebello, CA 96778
PROFESSIONAL SKILLS	Certified in First Aid/CPR Red Cross courses through advanced Certified Lifeguard/Advanced open water first aid for SCUBA Divers. Certified through SCUBA of America (1993)
REFERENCES	Available upon request

Figure 1-8: *Sample resume*

Returning the Application

After you have completed the application and are satisfied there are no spelling errors and every field is completed, return it in the same professional manner that you used to obtain it. While this is a time-consuming task, you will find that it pays dividends in the consideration your application will receive. You have shown that you are interested enough in the position to expend some effort to obtain it. If you have also acted in a professional manner and demonstrated your good manners, you will have made two good impressions on the agency before they even look at your qualifications. That, quite likely, is the first part of ***the edge*** you will need to meet their standards and obtain employment.

Summary

In this chapter, you learned how to determine where you would like to work. You then learned how to obtain an application and how to complete it. You also learned what type of resume to submit in the event the agency to whom you are applying requests one. Finally, you learned the best way to return the application to the agency from which you obtained it.

Learning Exercises

Where to Work?

Instructions: Project yourself ahead in time. You are now ready to look for a job with a law enforcement agency. Determine where you want to work.

To do this, use maps, descriptive literature, and anything else that can assist you in the decision-making process. If it is possible, visit the area or talk with someone who has been there.

Support your decision with a written report detailing the reasons you have chosen this specific area. Research deeply enough to find out what agencies serve the area and what job opportunities exist.

Filling Out an Application

Instructions: On the next three pages, you will find a sample application for employment. Complete the application using your own personal information. Fill in all of the blanks accurately, and do not omit any pertinent information. Follow instructions from your instructor for turning in the application.

Name ____________________

Social Security No. ____________________

Position ____________________

Testing Information

Written Exams Only:

Please indicate the location where you prefer to be tested.

- ☐ Boise
- ☐ Coeur d'Alene
- ☐ Idaho Falls
- ☐ Lewiston
- ☐ Pocatello
- ☐ Twin Falls

Boise Written Exams Only:

To the best of our ability we will test candidates at the time they prefer. Please mark your choice. Remember that because of hiring time frames we may not be able to honor your request.

- ☐ Saturday morning
- ☐ Weekday morning
- ☐ Weekday afternoon
- ☐ Weekday evening

Circle the Locations Where You Would Accept Employment:

STATEWIDE - Any

1 - Northern Idaho

All Cities in Northern Idaho
Athol
Bonners Ferry
Calder
Cataldo
Coeur d'Alene
Coolin
Harrison
Hayden
Kellogg
Kingston
Osburn
Pinehurst
Plummer
Priest River
St. Maries
Sandpoint
Santa
Spirit Lake
Wallace
Worley

2 - North Central Idaho

All Cities in No. Central Idaho
Ahsahka
Bovill
Cottonwood
Craigmont
Deary
Fleming
Grangeville
Kamiah
Kendrick
Kooskia
Lewiston
Lucile
Moscow
Orofino
Potlatch
Powell
Reeds Bar
Riggins
Weippe
Winchester

3 - Southwest Idaho

All Cities in Southwest Idaho
Banks
Boise
Bruneau
Caldwell
Cambridge
Cascade
Council
Eagle
Emmett
Glenns Ferry
Grand View
Homedale
Idaho City
Lowman
Marsing
McCall
Meridian
Mountain Home
Nampa
New Meadows
New Plymouth
Payette
Riddle
Weiser
Yellow Pine

4 - South Central Idaho

All Cities in So. Central Idaho
Almo
Bellevue
Bliss
Buhl
Burley
Carey
Fairfield
Filer
Gooding
Hagerman
Hailey
Jerome
Ketchum
Picabo
Rupert
Shoshone
Sublett
Twin Falls
Wendell

5 - Eastern Idaho

All Cities in Eastern Idaho
Aberdeen
American Falls
Ashton
Blackfoot
Downey
Driggs
Dubois
Grace
Idaho Falls
Irwin
Island Park
Malad City
Montpelier
Mud Lake
Paris
Pocatello
Preston
Rexburg
Rigby
Ririe
Roberts
St. Anthony
Soda Springs
Sterling
Sugar City
Swan Valley
Terreton
Victor
Wayan

6 - Central Idaho

All Cities in Central Idaho
Arco
Challis
Ellis
Gibbonsville
Mackay
Salmon
Stanley

STATE OF IDAHO EMPLOYMENT APPLICATION PC-1

Instructions:

1. Complete an application (PC-1) for each position desired.
2. Answer the questions on the reverse side of the announcement (Qualifications Statement PC-1.A) and submit with application. Place name and position applied for on each sheet. Sign application.
3. Submit the application enough in advance to insure it is received by midnight of the closing date. The Idaho Personnel Commission does not assume responsibility for delays in the mail or FAX transmissions. If an application is sent by FAX, please follow it with an original marked "Replacement Application." See below.
4. Please notify us if you move. Current address and phone numbers are essential to be called for an interview. Failure to do so will result in your name being removed from the list of eligible candidates.
5. **War Veterans:** To receive veterans' preference points, complete and enclose a Veterans' Preference Form (VP-1). VP-1s are available at Idaho Job Service offices and the Idaho Personnel Commission.
6. **Testing Accommodations:** To receive reasonable accommodations in testing for disability or religious reasons, complete a Testing Accommodations Request. The request forms are available at Idaho Job Service offices and the Idaho Personnel Commission. The testing accommodations information will be kept confidential.
7. Please keep a copy of your application material. The Idaho Personnel Commission does not make copies for applicants.

MAIL or FAX to:

Idaho Personnel Commission
700 West State Street
Boise, Idaho 83720-2700
FAX # (208) 334-3182

IDENTIFYING INFORMATION

Position Applied For (one only) ______________________

Announcement Number: ______________________

Social Security Number ☐☐☐-☐☐-☐☐☐☐

This application is for:
☐ New Application
☐ Retest
☐ Transfer of Score
☐ Extension of Score
☐ Replacement for FAXed Application

Mr☐ / Ms☐ ______________________
Last Name First Name Middle Initial

____
Mailing Address (Street or P.O. Box)

____
City / State / Zip

Other names used in past on State of Idaho applications: ______________________

( ) ______________________ ( ) ______________________
Home/Message Phone Work/Message Phone

Current State Employee? no ☐ yes ☐ If yes, which Department? ______________________

Do you want your application considered only by that Department? ☐ yes ☐ no

Conditions of Employment: Mark the types of employment you would accept.

yes no
☐ ☐ Full-time employment
☐ ☐ Part-time employment (less than 40 hrs/week)
☐ ☐ Temporary employment (cannot exceed 1385 hours in 12-month period)
☐ ☐ Seasonal employment (classified position with intermittent work periods throughout year)
☐ ☐ Night employment

yes no
☐ ☐ Shift employment
☐ ☐ Limited Service (classified, non-career positions of limited duration)
☐ ☐ 6-Month position (classified position, not to exceed 6 months)
☐ ☐ 9-Month position (classified position, not to exceed 9 months)

WHERE DID YOU FIND OUT ABOUT THIS POSITION?

☐ ALEX
☐ Direct Mailing
☐ Friend/Relative
☐ Idaho Personnel Commission
☐ Job Fair
☐ Job Service
☐ Newspaper
☐ Other State Agency
☐ Public Link
☐ Special Interest Group
☐ Trade Journal
☐ University/College Recruiter

7/93

EDUCATION Schools Attended After High School or Special Training Received

NAME	LOCATION City, State	FROM Mo/Yr	TO Mo/Yr	DID YOU GRADUATE?	TYPE OF DEGREE OR DIPLOMA
				☐ yes ☐ no	
				☐ yes ☐ no	
				☐ yes ☐ no	

Special Qualifications	Licensing

EXPERIENCE

EMPLOYMENT HISTORY: List your work history beginning with your present or most recent job.

Employer's Name and Address (Firm, Organization, etc.)	May We Contact This Employer? ☐ yes ☐ no	Phone No.	FROM Mo/Yr	TO Mo/Yr
Exact Title of Position	Supervisor's Name/Title		TOTAL TIME Yrs/Mos	HOURS/WEEK
Reason for Leaving				

Employer's Name and Address (Firm, Organization, etc.)	May We Contact This Employer? ☐ yes ☐ no	Phone No.	FROM Mo/Yr	TO Mo/Yr
Exact Title of Position	Supervisor's Name/Title		TOTAL TIME Yrs/Mos	HOURS/WEEK
Reason for Leaving				

Employer's Name and Address (Firm, Organization, etc.)	May We Contact This Employer? ☐ yes ☐ no	Phone No.	FROM Mo/Yr	TO Mo/Yr
Exact Title of Position	Supervisor's Name/Title		TOTAL TIME Yrs/Mos	HOURS/WEEK
Reason for Leaving				

Except for minor traffic offenses, have you ever entered a plea of guilty, no contest, or had a withheld judgment to any felony?

☐ yes ☐ no If YES, please explain.

Note: An affirmative answer to this question will not be an automatic bar to employment. Each situation will be evaluated on a case-by-case basis.

Signature ____________________ Please Print Last Name First Name Middle Initial	Date	Social Security No.

By my signature above, I certify that all answers and statements on this application are true and complete to the best of my knowledge. I understand that should an investigation disclose untruthful or misleading answers, my application may be rejected, my name removed from consideration, or my employment with the State terminated.

True/False Questions

Instructions: Circle the T if the statement is true, or circle the F if the statement is false.

T F 1. The best way to obtain an application for a position with a law enforcement agency is to phone and ask them to send you one.

T F 2. It is best to apply to several agencies at the same time when you are looking for an opening.

T F 3. Wear casual, sporty clothes when you pick up an application.

T F 4. If you are not sure of the dates of former employment, it is better to guess than to call a former employer to verify them.

T F 5. All information on an application will be carefully checked by the agency.

T F 6. Use a pencil to fill out an application so you can erase any errors.

T F 7. Withholding even minor information can cause you to wash out of the hiring process.

T F 8. It is acceptable to complete an application on the typewriter.

T F 9. It is important to keep a copy of the application for future reference.

T F 10. Negative information should be omitted from an application.

The Many Faces of Law Enforcement

There are many different areas of law enforcement in which a person can work. Although some specific duties may require a certain amount of job experience and tenure, other job assignments can be attained in a relatively short period of time. The following table lists some of the specific positions that any officer with the required amount of training and experience can work toward.

This list should not be considered complete because different agencies will always have different needs and *special assignments* for their geographical areas. This variation provides another good reason why you should research the agency for which you want to work to be sure they offer the assignments that interest you.

JOB TITLE	JOB DESCRIPTION
Supervisor, Commander, Department Manager	Supervise and regulate activities under their jurisdiction
Field Training Officer	Trains and teaches the new employees the policy and field tactics of the department
Special Enforcement Team	Confronts and deters a specific problem in the community such as an increase in robberies, burglaries, purse snatching, drug sales, etc. as it arises
Detective/Investigator	Investigates and solves reported crimes on which officers have initially taken the report
Police K-9 Handler	Uses a trained police dog to assist officers with the apprehension of suspected criminals and locating illegal activities

JOB TITLE	JOB DESCRIPTION
Evidence Technician/ Crime Scene Processor	Responds to the scene of a crime and conducts searches and collections for trace evidence. Also maintains control over evidence and properly logs it into an evidence room
Crime Scene Photographer	Photographs crime scenes
Narcotics Officer (Narc)	Enforces drug law violations through the use of covert drug purchases, surveillance, and search warrants
Traffic Enforcement	Assigned to strictly enforce traffic law violations
Anti-Gang Unit And Anti-Terrorist Unit	Assigned to curb gang violence in gang-proclaimed areas
Bicycle or Mounted Police	Teams patrol areas on bicycles or horses instead of patrol cars
Motorcycle Unit	Patrols on motorcycles for traffic violators
Fugitive Warrant Division	Locates and arrests fugitives who have failed to appear in court or have escaped from custody
Search and Rescue	Aids in locating lost and injured persons. Operates mostly in rural or mountainous areas
D.A.R.E. Instructor	Teaches school age children in the classroom how to avoid drug use and abuse
Neighborhood Watch Coordinator	Instructs groups of citizens how to organize crime watch programs

JOB TITLE	JOB DESCRIPTION
Aerial Surveillance/ Law Enforcement Pilot	Pilots an aircraft and observes while aiding ground units in searches and crimes in progress
Traffic Accident Investigator	Investigates major traffic accidents and those resulting in fatalities
Background Investigator	Investigates the backgrounds of prospective employees
Range Master	Maintains the department's firearms and weapon qualification for all officers
Self-Defense Instructor	Maintains the required continual self-defense training for employees
S.W.A.T. Team	Specially trained group that responds to extreme, high-risk encounters such as serving high-risk search or arrest warrants, hostage situations, and barricaded suspects
Dignitary Protection	Protects the well-being of high-profile persons

Field Officer

Photograph courtesy of Robert J. Piel

Officers respond to a domestic violence call and prepare to arrest the subject.

© 1996 Mark C. Ide

Officer engages in friendly chat with a small citizen.

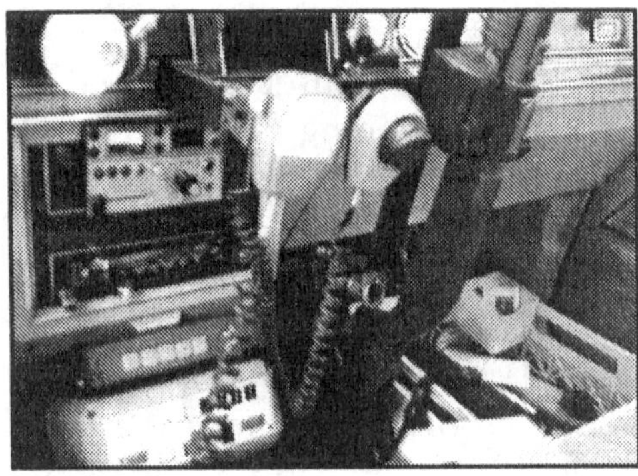
Photograph courtesy of Robert J. Piel

Interior of a typical squad car.

Photograph courtesy of Robert J. Piel

Officers respond to a stolen vehicle call and prepare to arrest the subject after a pursuit.

Accident Investigation

Photograph courtesy of Robert J. Piel

A suspect lies hancuffed on his stomach following a high speed pursuit. He was traveling in excess of 80 mph when he failed to negotiate a curve in the road. He survived. Officers discuss exactly how he crashed and where his motorcycle impacted the sidewalk.

© 1996 Mark C. Ide

Officers investigate a major traffic accident involving cars and a boat. Note the aerial surveillance helicopter and the emergency response team.

Photograph courtesy of Robert J. Piel

This officer checks for a pulse on a motorcycle crash victim. He was pronounced dead at the hospital 30 minutes later.

Aerial Surveillance

Photograph courtesy of Los Angeles, CA Police Department

Police helicopter pilot observing ground activities.

Anti-Gang Unit

Members of an Anti-Gang Unit readying to go on the streets to talk to youths.

S.W.A.T. Team

Members of a S.W.A.T. Team remove a suspect who had barricaded himself.

S.W.A.T. Team members subdue street violence.

Police K-9 Handler

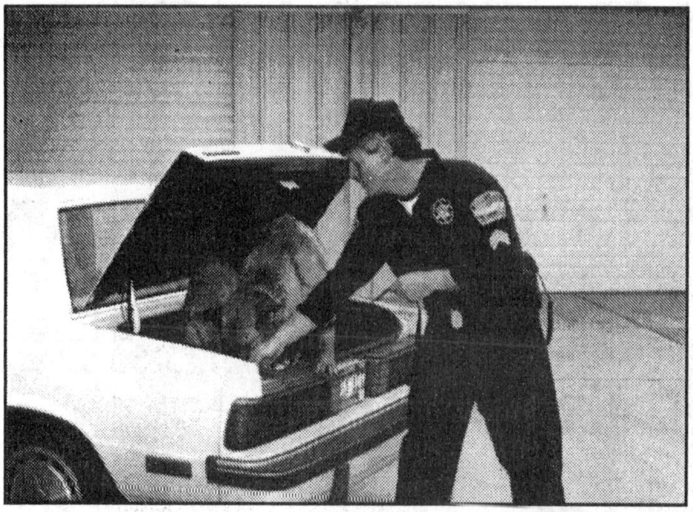

Photograph courtesy of Robert J. Piel

This officer and his dog are searching a suspect's vehicle for drugs. They were concealed in a panel of the trunk, but the dog found them.

Photograph courtesy of Robert J. Piel

Sheriff's officers and K-9 companion ready for a day in the field

Photograph courtesy of Robert J. Piel

K-9 officer attempting to apprehend a combative felon with aid from the dog.

Narcotics Officer

Photograph courtesy of Robert J. Piel

Photograph courtesy of Robert J. Piel

Narcotics officers discover a marijuana growing operation located in the forests of Northern Idaho.

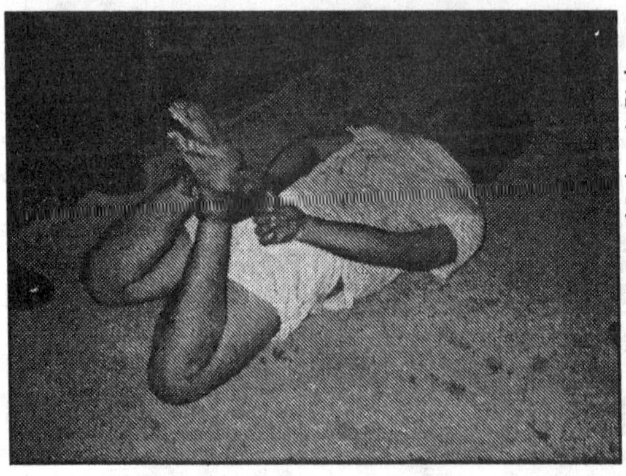
Photograph courtesy of Robert J. Piel

The subject lies stunned on the pavement after being shocked with a tazer gun. He was under the influence of PCP. Note the tazer wires and darts on his back.

Photograph courtesy of Robert J. Piel

An officer discovers methamphetamine hidden in a drug dealer's vehicle.

Search and Rescue

© 1996 Mark C. Ide

Search and Rescue team plans the strategy of the search.

© 1996 Mark C. Ide

Search and Rescue team organizes citizens to help locate a missing ten year-old child.

© 1996 Mark C. Ide

Charity Activities

© 1996 Mark C. Ide

Police-sponsored boxing match to aid disadvantaged

In Memorium

Officers gather to pay their respects to a fallen comrade.

Member of a Mounted Patrol escorts the hearse.

Memorial Services for slain police officers, Westboro, MA

Chapter Two
The Written Exam

Objectives

When you have completed this chapter, you will understand:

1. That all candidates for positions in law enforcement must take a written examination
2. These examinations will test your basic math and vocabulary skills as well as your ability to record events accurately and in detail
3. How to prepare for these written examinations by reviewing before you take them
4. Where to obtain materials that may be useful in your review

Key Terms

- written examination
- civil service examination
- observation skills

Introduction

Now that you have submitted your application to several agencies, you will have to wait for them to make the next move. The agencies will process your application. Because this can be time consuming, don't worry if you don't hear anything right away. Sometimes it takes several weeks.

written examination: written tests given by a law enforcement agency to determine if applicants meet certain qualifications

If your application is accepted, a notice will be sent to you giving the date and time of the next **written examination** for all eligible applicants. Passing the written exam is the next step in the hiring process.

Figure 2-1: *Receiving the notice for the written exam*

Before You Take the Examination

Before you take the exam, you should spend some time learning about it. Most law enforcement agencies use a standard **civil service examination**. The questions are usually multiple choice, and a time limit is placed on the test. Several study books are available that are designed to acquaint the reader with civil service tests. They can be found in most libraries or purchased at book stores.

civil service examination: a test given to applicants for jobs in public service

Career Publishing Inc., publisher of this book, offers many types of review videotapes. Included are ones for both the civil service exams and police officer exams. Even if you have taken a civil service test before and think you know all about it, just remember a refresher never hurt anyone. When you are adequately prepared, you can face the testing more confidently.

When you are ready to start studying, find a quiet place and get comfortable — but not too comfortable. You want to study, not sleep. Make notes about the contents of the book as you read.

Figure 2-2: *Applicant studying for the written exam*

If you come across a word that you do not understand, look it up in the dictionary. Write down the word, and use it in a sentence of your own. This will help you remember the word.

If you use the civil service study books, go over the sample tests before you begin to read the book to get an idea of what they are like. Then take the sample tests several times, so that you become familiar with the way the questions are worded. Do not check in the back of the book to see if your answers are correct until after you have finished taking the test. Then check your answers.

Taking the Examination

When you receive notice of the date and time of the exam, make sure you arrive on time. The agency will not delay or postpone the exam. It will be given as scheduled.

Try to get plenty of rest the night before the exam, so that you are refreshed and alert. Make sure you eat a good breakfast the day of the test. Dress professionally, but try to be comfortable also.

Figure 2-3: *Eat a good breakfast on the day you take the written exam*

Bring a pen and pencil with you; they may not be supplied. Most tests require that the answers be marked with a #2 lead pencil. While you are taking the test, do not change an answer unless you are absolutely sure the answer you have marked is wrong. Several expert test professionals have stated that your first choice is usually correct unless you are positive you have made an error.

Figure 2-4: *Examiner giving applicants instructions*

Before you begin to take the test, the examiner will give you instructions. Listen carefully. This may help you to avoid making a mistake. At the top of the exam will be examples that show you how to answer the questions on the exam. Read these examples carefully before you begin.

Remember this is a timed exam. When you are answering the questions, skip those that are difficult for you and return to them later.

When you have finished the exam, go over it again to check your work and make sure you have answered all the questions. If you did not complete a question because you were unsure of the answer, do not leave it blank. A question without an answer is always wrong. Guess if you have to. You have a chance of getting it right if you guess; no chance if you leave it blank.

Sample Questions

The civil service examination will test your math and vocabulary in a number of ways. You will be tested on spelling, word meanings, grammar, and reading comprehension. You will be given sample problems that stress the practical applications of whole numbers, fractions, percentages, and decimals. The next section contains some sample questions similar to those you will encounter in the civil service exam.

Name ____________________
Date ____________________
SS # ____________________

Vocabulary

Instructions: Each of the following statements has a key word. It appears in bold print. The object of the questions is to see if the word is used properly in a sentence. Circle the T if it is used correctly or F if it is not used correctly.

T F 1. An **inquisitive** child is one who never asks questions.

T F 2. A person who **procrastinates** will get the job done quickly.

T F 3. To **belie** your name is to give it falsely.

T F 4. If you **acknowledge** someone, you recognize them.

T F 5. An **accomplice** is one who aids in the commission of a crime.

T F 6. An **acquaintance** should be considered a close friend.

T F 7. **Prejudice**, in simple terms, means bias.

Reading Comprehension

Instructions: After reading the following paragraph, decide which answer describes the paragraph more accurately than the other answers. Circle the letter of the correct answer.

As the officer progressed in his training, his knowledge and skill greatly enhanced his ability to perform the job. Had it not been for his dedication to the profession, he might still be walking a beat. He has climbed the ladder of success within his department and has used his experience to help train other officers.

Which of the following sentences best describes this paragraph?
A. The officer does not like walking a beat.
B. Being a dedicated professional helps you and makes training easier.
C. The officer used what he had learned to advance in his department.
D. If you have training, knowledge, and skill you can climb ladders.

Name ____________________
Date ____________________
SS # ____________________

Math

1. Draw a right angle. __________
2. Divide 764,348 by 102. __________
3. 3/4 + 1/2 - 1/8 =__________.
4. Write .75 as a percent? __________
5. 7865 x 5687 =__________.
6. An officer writes 24 tickets each month. If 1/2 of the tickets are for speeding, what percentage of the tickets are for other violations? __________

Other Testing Procedures

Many agencies will also *customize* the written examinations by incorporating their own testing procedures. For example, a person may abruptly enter the room, create some type of commotion, and then quickly leave. You may think nothing of it until the end of the test when an instructor asks you to write down a complete description of the subject who walked past you two hours ago. That could be difficult if you did not pay attention to what was going on around you. Practice your **observation skills** all the time.

observation skills: being able to look at someone or something and remember many details in order to give an accurate description

Another common test of observation skills may simply be having the instructor show every applicant a photograph as they enter the room. At the end of the examination they will be asked to write a description of what they observed in the picture.

Figure 2-5: *Examiner showing applicants a picture*

In any case, be ready for the unexpected. Here are some ways to sharpen your observation skills.

- Use your television set
- Observe people and cars closely
- Practice, practice, practice

Turn on your television to a local news station. Look at the news anchor person or persons for about five or ten seconds. Pay close attention to their hair style, jewelry on their hands, neck, or clothing, and anything else that will help them stand out in your memory. Then leave the room for ten minutes.

After that time and while you are still in the other room, sit down and write everything you can recall about the physical appearance of the person(s) you observed on television. After you write your description on a piece of paper, return to the television and check your accuracy.

Figure 2-6: *Applicant taking the written exam*

Write down the description of a friend's car. Try to remember scratches, dents, or any other information that could help to identify it and the location of the damage. The next time you see that vehicle, look at your written description and compare.

The most important thing to remember is that observation skills get better with practice and experience. If you want to compete favorably with other applicants for a job in law enforcement, you must be prepared to practice sharpening different skills all the time.

If you are applying with a city police department or the county sheriff, expect to write some type of hypothetical (pretend) incident report. Here are a few tips.

- Do not use any police jargon.
- Do not abbreviate any words.
- Write in plain, simple English using the first person.

For example:

REPORT

Officer responding ____________________

Date ____________________

ON JANUARY 1, 1995, I RESPONDED TO THE REPORT OF AN INJURY VEHICLE ACCIDENT AT 0000 FIFTH STREET. WHEN I ARRIVED, I LOCATED THE DRIVERS AND DIS-COVERED THAT THERE WERE NO INJURIES. I CAN-CELED THE RESPONDING AMBULANCE AND HAD THE DRIVERS MOVE THEIR VEHICLES OUT OF THE TRAFFIC LANES.

The purpose of this exercise is to test your writing skills, not to see if you know how to write a crime report. Print the report using uppercase letters, and check your spelling. If you can't spell a word correctly, or you think it may be misspelled, choose an easier word that has the same meaning to use in its place.

As you can see, the tests are not particularly hard, but they do require the applicant to use common sense, have a good general knowledge base, and practical mathematical skills.

Summary

In this chapter, you learned that applicants for a job in law enforcement must pass certain written tests as the next step in obtaining that position. They must have basic math and vocabulary abilities and be able to record events accurately and in detail. You also learned that you should review before taking these tests. Sources of review books and videos for civil service examinations were presented.

Learning Activities

Reviewing with the Buddy System

Have each student pick a buddy with whom they can review for the written examinations. If possible, the buddy should be chosen from the class. Have them take turns asking and answering the types of questions they are likely to encounter on the exam. Have them plan to continue this reviewing until both of them are satisfied they know the material.

Additional Sample Questions

Vocabulary

Instructions: Pick the word that is closest in meaning to the sample word.

1. Omnipotent: (A) Hidden
(B) All-powerful
(C) Kind
(D) Ever-present

2. Sagacious: (A) Discerning
(B) Talkative
(C) Cruel
(D) Presentable

3. Vacillate: (A) Forthright
(B) Innoculate
(C) Waver
(D) Resolute

4. Amplify: (A) Expand
(B) Postpone
(C) Kindle
(D) Exaggerate

5. Resuscitate: (A) Resist
(B) Suffocate
(C) Attack
(D) Revive

Instructions: In each pair of sentences, one is correct and one is incorrect. Circle the letter of the incorrect sentence.

1. a. The earth revolves around the sun in an orbit.
   b. Neither the earth nor the other planets was revolving around the moon.

2. a. Mr. Jones, my dad's best friend, who I had not seen in a long time, knocked on the door.
   b. He, along with his wife, is going on an island cruise.

3. a. Each of the boys has to feed their own dog.
   b. He was dependable in doing his chores.

Spelling

Instructions: Circle the word that is incorrectly spelled in each group.

1. (A) Wierd (C) Heinous
   (B) Cieling (D) Mischief

2. (A) Movable (C) Changeable
   (B) Admirable (D) Acknowledgable

3. (A) Occurrence (C) Ommitted
   (B) Accomodate (D) Committed

4. (A) Intercede (C) Superceed
   (B) Suburb (D) Intervene

5. (A) Inference (C) Remitance
   (B) Reference (D) Occurrence

Math

1. A mailing machine can address 2,000 envelopes in 5 minutes. How many hours will it take to address 149,000 envelopes?

2. Kathy earned $8 per hour for the first 40 hours she worked and $12 per hour for each additional hour. If she earned $416 in one week, how many hours did she work?

3. If five word processors can enter a manuscript in three days, how many days will it take two word processors to do the same job?

4. A basketball team played 140 games and won 90 of them. What was the ratio of the number of games lost to the number of games won?

5. If Bill's business is assessed at $65,000, how much tax will he pay at the rate of $45 per $1,000?

6. Over the past ten years, crime rates in a certain city have increased by 200%. If the rate ten years ago was 4 per 1,000, what is the rate today?

7. Five is 25% of what number?

8. Reduce 22/48 to the lowest terms.

9. If one box of toys weighs 3 1/3 pounds, how many pounds do 125 boxes weigh?

10. Change 3/4 to a decimal.

True/False Questions

T F 1. Most law enforcement agencies use a standard Civil Service written test.

T F 2. You can locate a copy of the Civil Service test to study at your local library.

T F 3. It helps to watch television while you are studying for the written test.

T F 4. Unless you are sure your answer is wrong, you should not change your first answer.

T F 5. If you do not know some of the answers, leave them blank.

T F 6. Most written tests will test your ability to read, write, and solve math problems.

T F 7. If you come across a word that you do not understand while studying, look up its meaning in the dictionary.

T F 8. All agencies use the same testing format.

T F 9. Practicing observation skills will not help during the written test.

T F 10. If you are asked to write a police report for the test, you should use as many *police words* as possible.

Chapter Three
The Physical Agility Test

Objectives

When you have completed this chapter, you will understand:

1. The physical requirements for becoming a law enforcement officer
2. Which exercises will help you strengthen your body
3. The value of following a structured training program
4. The agility tests you will have to satisfactorily pass

Key Terms

- physical agility
- cardiovascular
- stamina

Introduction

The physical agility test is a basic test of your physical fitness. You will be required to pass several tests. If you are in good physical condition, this should not be a problem. However, if you are out of shape, there is only one thing you can do. Exercise! Exercise! Exercise! to get into shape.

stamina: endurance

Stamina and upper body strength are very important for anyone in law enforcement. if you find this hard to believe, just imagine yourself having to chase a criminal for half a mile, climbing over three six-foot fences, and then ending your pursuit with a tackle that would make most professional football players envious.

A Life Saver

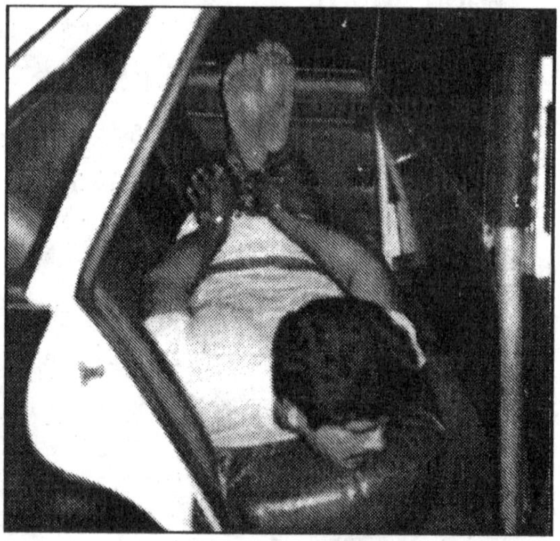

Figure 3-1: *Subject under the influence of PCP struggled with the arresting officer but was succesfully subdued*

Now imagine this realistic scenario. You finally catch this person only to find that you are too tired to defend yourself. So the criminal, who has been bench pressing four hundred pounds in prison every day, gets to make the decision whether you live or die. Let's hope he's in a good mood, for your family's sake.

Now, let's look at an alternate solution. After your wild pursuit, you finally tackle the criminal. You find he is a mighty opponent because of his excellent physical conditioning. However, you also are in excellent shape and soon subdue him. That evening you return to your family tired but safe.

Getting in Shape

There are several simple exercises you can do to increase your upper body strength. Push-ups, pull-ups, bar dips and, of course, weight training will all improve it. When you begin **cardiovascular** exercises, they should be limited to about 20 minutes every other day until you are accustomed to the exercise. Running, bicycle riding (mobile and stationary), walking at a brisk pace, and using stairstepping machines are excellent ways to improve your stamina.

cardiovascular: involving the heart and blood vessels

Most public gyms have trainers who will help you get started on a training program. Tell them about your plans, and they will prepare a workout program suited to your needs. It is best if you have been following a structured training program for approximately four weeks before you submit your application. This period of time will help to assure your readiness for the **physical agility test.**

Nutrition also plays a very important part in helping you to maintain your stamina. Always try to eat a well balanced diet.

The Physical Agility Test

physical agility test: a measure of your ability to perform specified exercises easily

The night before your agility test, get plenty of rest. You will do better if you do not have a big breakfast on the morning of the test. A more suitable breakfast might be a small portion of fresh fruit, one piece of wheat toast, and a glass of nonfat milk. This should supply you with an adequate amount of energy to perform the test.

Figure 3-2: *Choices for a suitable breakfast*

Preparing for the

Simulated Bar Dips

Down Position

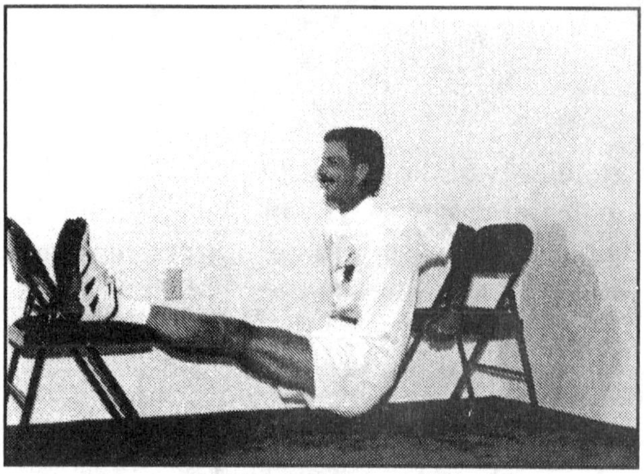

Up Position

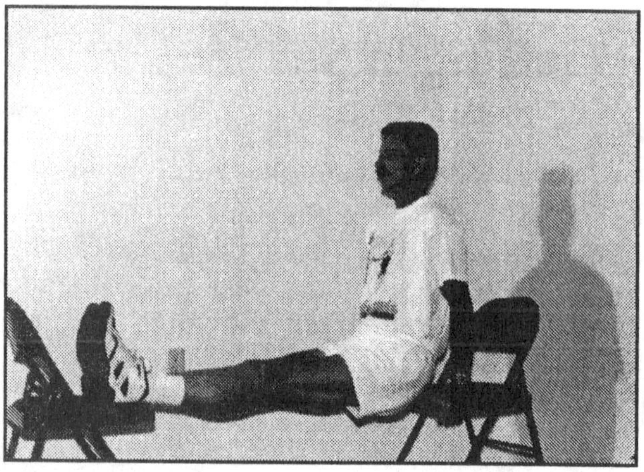

Sit-Ups

Down Position

Up Position

Push-Ups

Down Position

Up Position

Physical Agility Test

Pull-Ups

Down Position

Up Position

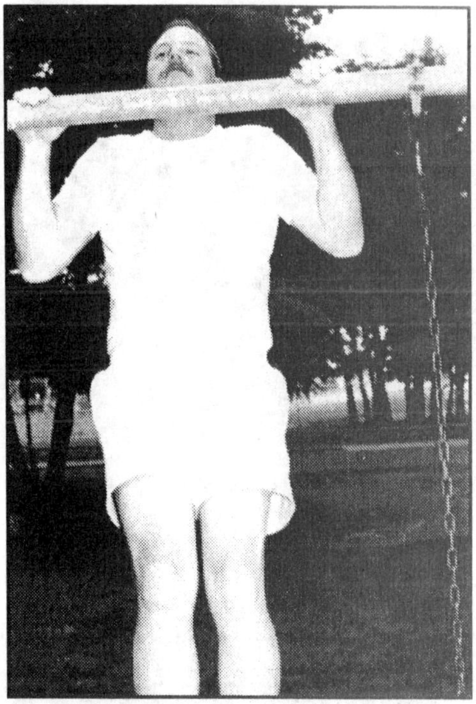

Body Drag

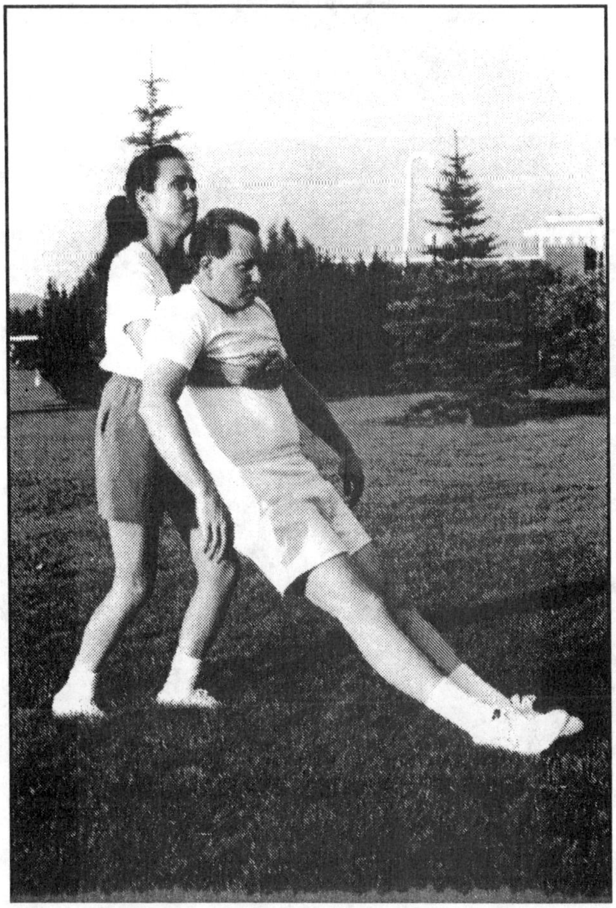

Running on a Home Treadmill

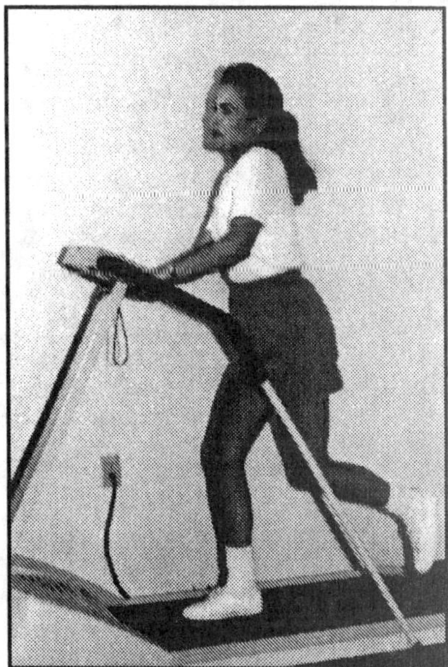

Photographs courtesy of Robert J. Piel

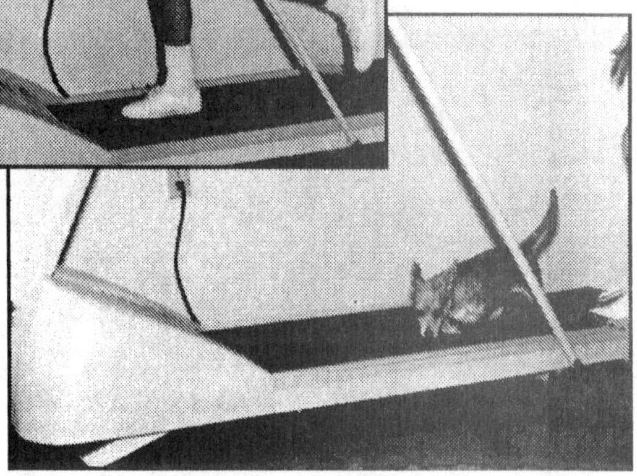

Even Fido gets into the act

Applicant performing the coordination test while running the obstacle course

Upper body strength test during the obstacle course

Photographs courtesy of Robert J. Piel

Applicant engaged in the 1.5 mile run

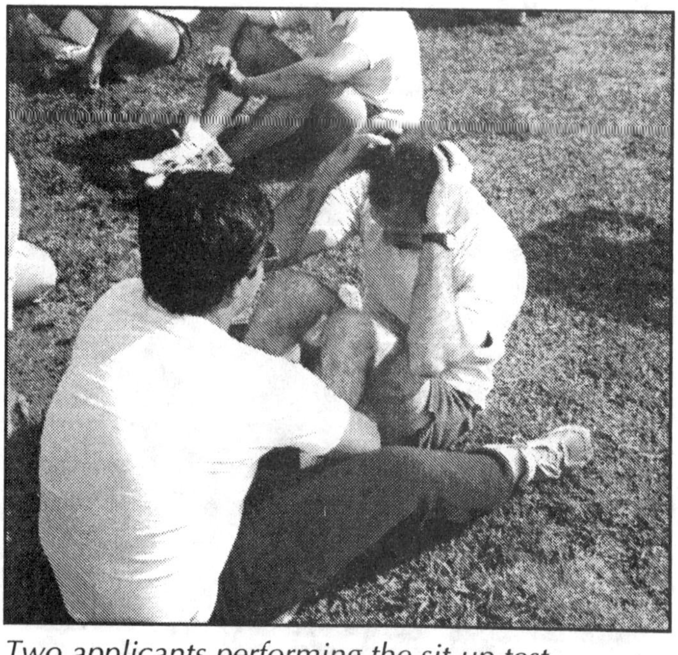

Two applicants performing the sit-up test

Physical Agility Test

Rio Hondo Police Academy, Whittier, California

Actual physical agility test preparing to start

Police Sergeant describing the obstacle course for the group

Applicant scaling the seven foot wall while running the obstacle course

Plan to arrive at the location where the test is scheduled about twenty minutes before the test. Use this time to stretch and warm up. This exercise will reduce the risk of injury. You cannot pass the test if you cannot perform the exercises. The following are some of the more common agility tests that are used by law enforcement agencies today.

- Run 1-1/4 to 1-1/2 miles within a certain time limit, usually about 13 to 15 minutes.
- Run an obstacle course within a certain time limit, usually approximately 45 to 60 seconds.
- Climb over a 6- or 7-foot wall or fence.
- Drag a 150 lb. object 50 feet.
- Do five pull-ups.

You can prepare for several of these tests ahead of time. To prepare for running, practice on a local high school or college track. Most of these are 1/4-mile tracks. Carry a stop watch, and time yourself. You can also practice running on a home treadmill. You can practice dragging a 150 pound object by having one of your friends play dead while you drag them across a grass field. If you have access to an obstacle course, practice running it.

Doing five pull-ups is probably the most difficult test. However, being able to accomplish this test indicates that it is likely you have the required upper body strength to perform in law enforcement. When you are tested, you may find that several of these tests are combined. You may be asked to run one mile, climb a wall and then have to pull a dummy 50 feet. Be prepared, and remember you will not be the only person taking this test, so you must give 110 percent of yourself.

If you find that you cannot perform any of these tests easily, you may wish to postpone applying until your physical condition has improved. It is much better to postpone applying than to apply and fail the physical agility examination.

It is very important that you discuss your ability to perform these exercises with your local doctor. He or she should give you a complete physical examination to ensure you are in the proper condition to begin training. If you find you have a recurring problem or a pain that persists while you are training, we suggest that you contact a sports medicine physician. This doctor has been specially trained and will be well prepared to assist you through the training program.

Summary

In this chapter, you learned the physical requirements for becoming a law enforcement officer and which exercises help you most to strengthen your body, as well as the specific physical agility tests you will have to satisfactorily pass. You also learned the value of good nutrition and following a structured training program.

Learning Activities

True/False Questions

If the statement is true, circle the T. If the statement is false, circle the F.

T F 1. Warming up before the physical agility test will not help pass the test.

T F 2. Eating a light breakfast an hour or two before the test is a good idea.

T F 3. Being in poor physical shape will not matter during physical agility test because you can get in shape after you enter the training academy.

T F 4. You should drink a lot of water before the agility test so you do not become dehydrated.

T F 5. You should practice running an obstacle course before the test to identify the areas in which you need to improve.

T F 6. If you have good upper body strength, it will help you pass the physical agility test.

T F 7. Push-ups and pull-ups are good ways to increase upper body strength.

T F 8. You should stretch after the agility test, but not before the test.

T F 9. Exercising on stair machines and stationary bicycles helps to increase physical stamina.

T F 10. The physical agility test may require you to perform several types of physical tests in a row.

Chapter Four
The Oral Interview

Objectives

When you have completed this chapter, you will understand:

1. How to prepare for the oral interview
2. What to expect during the oral interview
3. The types of questions you will be asked
4. The best type of response to the questions
5. The difference between a nonstress interview and a stress interview
6. The correct way to respond to hypothetical situations

Key Terms

- hypothetical situation
- stress interview
- nonstress interview

Introduction

The oral interview is perhaps the most important part of the hiring process. You will come face to face with the people who are doing the hiring. You will be required to talk about yourself and answer any questions they may ask. This can be a very nerve-wracking experience, and how you present yourself is very important.

Preparing for the Interview

Before you have your interview, write a short autobiography and tell about yourself. Include not only those things asked on your application, such as the places you have worked and the schools you have attended, but also tell other things about yourself. The agency to which you are applying is going to want to know the *person* they are hiring. What are the things you like to do? What are your hobbies? Who are your friends? How do you spend your free time? Include all of these things in your autobiography. Then spend time reading it to yourself. How does it sound? What can you change to make it sound better? Then practice saying what you have written. Do not try to memorize what you have written, but familiarize yourself with it.

Figure 4-1: *Writing an autobiography*

There are several ways to practice. One way is to sit in front of a mirror as if you were speaking to the oral board. Record what you are saying, and then play it back. Listen carefully not only to the words, but also to the tone of voice you are using. Do you sound uncertain or are you confident? Does your voice sound friendly? If this were a stranger's voice, would it inspire your confidence?

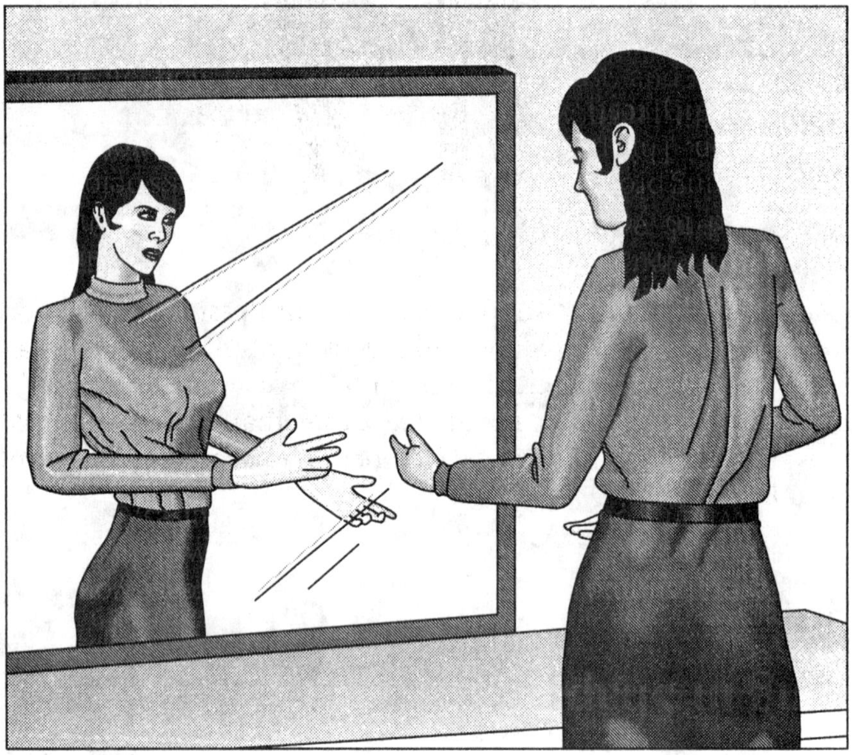

Figure 4-2: *Practicing for the oral interview*

Again, make any changes that will improve what you are saying. Remember, you are going to *sell* yourself to these people. If you are sure of yourself and confident in your answers, it will show. Do not take this part of the process lightly. It is a very important step.

The oral interview generally lasts from fifteen minutes to an hour. There is no way to predict how long your interview will last, and some have lasted more than an hour. The length of the interview usually does not have a bearing on how the interviewers feel about you.

Later in this chapter, we will give you some sample questions you may expect to be asked during the oral interview, but for now we will work on the interview. You have written an autobiography and rehearsed what you are going to say about yourself.

Figure 4-3: *Dress appropriately for the interview*

Does what you wear matter? Yes, it does. Dress professionally. Do not arrive for the interview in a pair of jeans and a T-shirt. Men should wear a suit or sport coat with a tie and be clean shaven or have a neatly trimmed beard. Some agencies do not allow facial hair other than a mustache. Women should wear a nice pantsuit or dress. Do not put on a lot of makeup, and style your hair conservatively.

The Interview

Arrive for the interview a few minutes early. If you smoke, try to refrain from smoking before the interview. The smell of tobacco smoke lingers on your clothes, and although you cannot be disqualified for smoking, it may be offensive to one or more of the interviewers. This can cause them to give you a lower score. Drink coffee in moderation. The caffeine in coffee can make you nervous, and you will probably be nervous enough without adding caffeine. Do not chew gum, eat mints or candy, or have anything else in your mouth during the interview.

Figure 4-4: *Wait until after the interview for cigarettes, gum, and candy*

When you are called into the interview, introduce yourself to each of the interviewers. Shake their hands and repeat their names as they tell them to you. When you sit down, sit up straight, pull your chair in and keep your hands on your lap. When an interviewer asks a question, answer not to that person alone but to the entire panel. Look at each of them while you answer.

Figure 4-5: *Shake hands with the interviewers as you introduce yourself*

If you are asked a yes or no question, answer with "Yes sir" and "Yes ma'am," or "No sir" and "No ma'am." Many of the questions you will be asked may have several answers. Be brief and honest with your answers. Stick to your answer if you feel it is right even though the interviewers may try to persuade you to change your mind.

The following are some sample questions you may be asked during your interview. Each question is followed by a suggested response.

1. **Briefly tell us about yourself?**

   Take a deep breath, and then start by describing where you were born, the size of your family, the type of community you lived in, where you attended school, your hobbies, etc. Remember to describe your life in chronological order, and try not to jump back and forth when describing specific events. Keep your answer to three or four minutes. When you practice ahead of time, you learn how much you can say in that amount of time. As previously mentioned, have your answers well thought out and fresh in your mind.

2. **Why do you want to work with our agency?**

   Most people who wish to work in law enforcement have a common goal: *to help other people.* There is nothing wrong with this answer, but try to be more specific, and thus a little more convincing, by describing the events in your life that led you to aspire to a career in law enforcement. It will also help if you can describe why you are attracted to this particular agency. If you do some research about the agency before you apply, it will be easy to find the unique attributes associated with the agency.

3. **Do you know how many officers we employ?**

   While you may not know the exact number, you should be able to give an approximate answer.

4. **Do you know the name of our mayor?**

   If you have done your homework, you will.

5. **Do you know the name of our chief (or the highest ranking official)?**

   Not only should you know his or her name, you should know something about their tenure in office. You may not need this additional information during the interview, but it will be an added pillow of confidence.

6. **What is the ethnic percentage breakdown of our city (or area to which you will be assigned)?**

   Here again, you may not have exact figures, but you should have a pretty accurate general picture. It may also help if you understand where each group is located, or if the population is mixed throughout the area.

7. **Do you know the size in square miles of the area to which you will be assigned?**

   Do your homework and you will.

8. **Are you prepared to work alternating shifts and early morning hours?**

   I hope you realize before you consider a career in law enforcement that it will probably require your working at all hours of the day and night. Law enforcement is on duty twenty-four hours a day, and someone has to work the *off hours.*

9. **How can you benefit our agency?**

   Tell about the good qualities you possess; e.g., you have good writing skills and an above average command of the English language; you can speak another language; you are willing to commit to a long-term career with their agency, etc.

10. **Describe any training or knowledge you have or experience you possess that will assist your work in our agency?**

    If you do not have any prior experience in this field, then consider taking a few administration of justice or criminology classes at a local college. At best, if you can say you are currently enrolled at a local college, it shows that your interest in law enforcement is more than an *overnight dream.*

Eliminating the Unsuitable Applicants

Law enforcement agencies receive millions of applications every year from people commonly referred to as *wanna-be's.* This term is a slang expression that describes a person who wants to wear a badge and carry a gun just to feel important. He or she has no other reason for wishing to enter the law enforcement profession. Obviously, agencies must weed out these applicants from the more qualified ones. This is one of the purposes of the difficult hiring process.

There is no doubt that, on occasion, a *bad apple* slips through the process. We read about them in the newspaper or see them on the local television news. They are the officers who are arrested for theft, excessive force, and, on occasion, rape and murder. It is embarrassing to all of us in law enforcement when these incidents happen, so we wish to keep them to a minimum.

Figure 4-6: *Never consider law enforcement as a profession if it is because you think wearing a badge and carrying a gun will make you feel important*

4-10

Perhaps now would be a good time for you to examine your motivation for wishing to launch a career in this field. Be honest with yourself. There is nothing wrong with getting excited about this job. As a matter of fact, if you are not excited about it, you have no business applying. Take the time to examine your motivation carefully and assure yourself that the authority associated with carrying a gun is not the reason you are applying.

Community-Oriented Policing

Community-Oriented Policing, or **Community-Based Policing**, which is commonly referred to as **C.O.P.**, is a law enforcement philosophy that has gained momentum across the country. For the most part, this philosophy has peaked, with most municipal police departments adopting some aspect of it. We will start by explaining what C.O.P. is. In simple terms, C.O.P. is the forming of a partnership between law enforcement officers and the community they serve.

Community-Oriented Policing (C.O.P.): The forming of a partnership between law enforcement officers and the community they serve

This partnership can be formed in several different ways. For the most part, all that is needed is for the officer to keep close ties with his or her particular community. An officer usually will be assigned to work in an area or district consistently. This allows him or her to learn about the people in that area. This day-to-day contact, in return, will result in a more personal relationship between the police and the community.

Many law enforcement agencies encourage, if not require, their officers to live within the city limits of the area they serve. A C.O.P.-involved agency also will encourage officers to establish relationships with citizens and local merchants. The agency will encourage officers to become involved in neighborhood concerns and attend neighborhood meetings. They will promote interaction between the local schools and the officers. This Community Oriented Policy allows more discretion when making decisions that will affect the community because it acknowledges the impact on the people involved.

Part of the C.O.P. plan is to have officers feel a sense of responsibility toward a particular community, and with that in mind, be able to more directly solve problems. C.O.P.-minded agencies espouse the belief that *field operations patrol* is the *backbone* of the department, and every other division's purpose is to support and assist this group.

Because policing philosophies often evolve in cycles and are governed by community desires, we can reasonably conclude that C.O.P. will change shape and possibly no longer be the best solution for maintaining law and order in the years to come. However, for the present, it is the most current and viable method, and you should be prepared for it to affect you as a new police officer.

During the oral interview, expect to answer questions and render opinions regarding Community Oriented Policing. Be prepared to do a little research and find out how C.O.P. is viewed by the agency that is testing you. Be prepared to give a personal definition of C.O.P. to the oral board members and what you perceive is your role within the definition.

The key point to keep in mind is that C.O.P. is *the forming of a partnership between a law enforcement agency and the community they serve.*

Hypothetical Questioning

hypothetical situation: one subject to conjecture or supposition

Now it is time to get into the difficult area of questions about hypothetical situations during the oral interview. Most oral board interviewers have a preplanned set of hypothetical questions. Expect to be asked five to ten questions. These questions will always apply to the type of law enforcement your chosen agency deals with, such as drug enforcement, alcohol, tobacco and firearms, local police, sheriff, etc. Each applicant will be asked the same set of questions, and the answers will be given a numerical score.

We will begin by using the type of hypothetical questions a large county sheriff's office may ask. For example, it is your first day on the job and you are assigned to work with a training deputy. His or her job is to teach you how to write reports, investigate crimes, and all the other duties you will be required to perform. Your first radio call is the report of a theft at a local convenience store. While at the store, you observe your partner taking a candy bar and a package of cigarettes from a display rack and placing them in his or her pocket. You realize the clerk did not witness this, and your partner leaves the store without paying for the items. What are you going to do?

If you respond to this question by simply stating, "I would immediately report the incident to a superior," you are on the right track. If the interviewers do not have follow-up questions to your answer, then this is considered a ***nonstress oral interview.*** However, if they ask you follow-up questions, stand by for a ***stress oral interview,*** which is tough.

nonstress oral interview: one in which your answers will not have follow-up questions

stress oral interview: one in which your answers will be followed by more what-if questions on the same subject

Figure 4-7: *Applicant being interviewed for a position with a law enforcement agency*

We will continue by pretending that you are in a stress interview. The chances are the interviewers will begin to compound the original question by adding *what ifs.* For example, "You decide to confront your partner. What if he or she defends himself or herself by saying, 'Lots of us have arrangements with the local merchants. We give them prompt service, and they let us have free food and coffee. When you have finished training, you can get the free stuff too.'"

"What would you do now? Would you still report the incident to a superior?"

Now the question is a little more difficult. Do you change your answer? Are you beginning to second guess yourself? Let's say you decide to stick with your original answer and report the deputy to a superior. Now one of the more quiet interviewers yells at you.

"What if the sergeant or captain tells you to mind your own business or face the prospect of being fired! What are you going to do now?"

Now the pressure is on, and you are starting to panic. Take a deep breath and try not to get upset. The interviewers are simply testing your integrity. They want to see if you can be pressured into making the wrong decision. We cannot answer the questions for you, but keep this in mind: Are you a thief? Hopefully not. Do you want to work with a group of thieves? No! Stick to your answer, no matter what the surrounding circumstances appear to be.

If it gets to the point where the interviewers tell you the highest ranking official in the department does not care if members of the agency steal from local merchants, then this is not a place where you want to work anyway. Do not be afraid to tell them this is not the place for you — if they push the question that far.

Are you starting to see the picture now? The real question they are asking is not, "Would you steal or condone stealing if the circumstances permit?" It is, "Do you have integrity? Do you have pride? At what point do you say it's OK to steal?" Of course, your answer is simple. "Never!"

These interviewers are experienced interrogators. Refuse to allow their pressure or intimidation to persuade you to change your answer. Above all, remember this. The interviewers are no better than you. They are just trying to make sure you meet their expectations of honesty, pride, and integrity. If you give *wishy-washy* answers, they simply will have no need for you in their field. As previously mentioned, you have seen the news. One bad apple is too many for a smaller agency.

Sometimes the interviewers will move to another pressure question while you are still thinking about the first one. Again, it is a technique to see how you handle yourself under pressure. Take a deep breath, put the last question behind you, and listen to the next question.

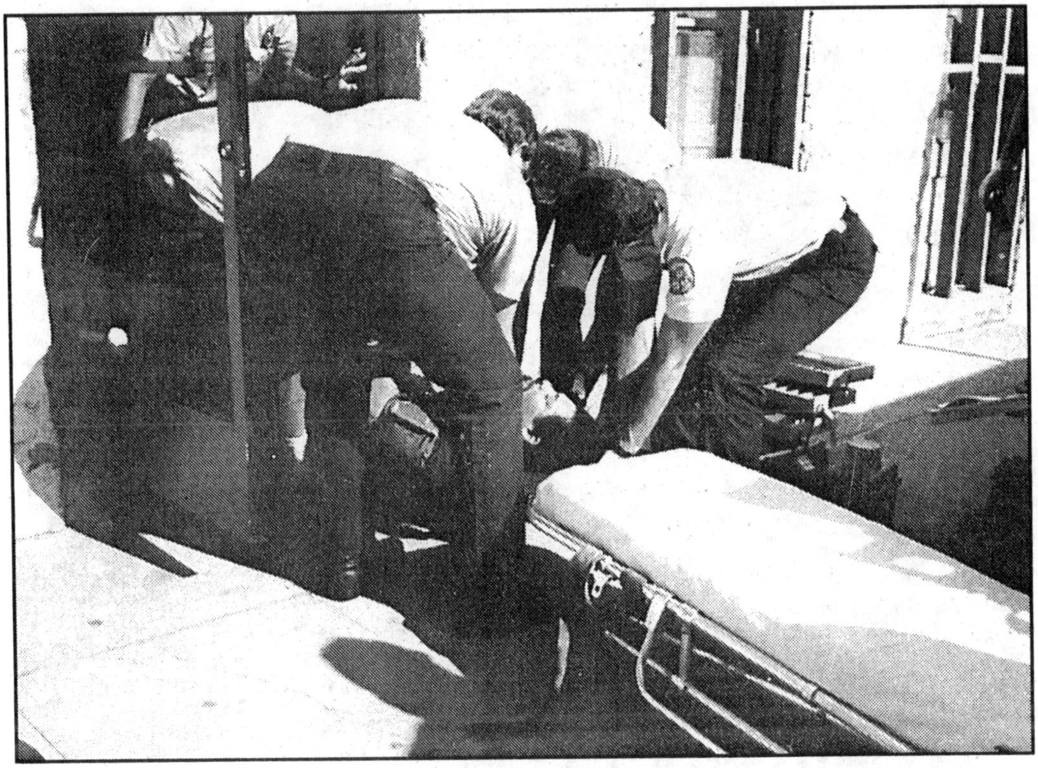

Figure 4-8: *Paramedics carrying a gunshot victim to a waiting ambulance*

You and your partner respond to a *man with a gun* call. Upon your arrival, this deranged screaming man jumps out of some bushes and pulls your partner's gun from the holster. At the same time, the man shields himself with your partner's body and holds the gun to your partner's head. The man is screaming about Martians from outer space attacking our planet and how he must kill a police officer to save the world. He is sweating profusely, and it appears he is going to shoot your partner. You have a split second to react. What are you going to do?

Before you can answer the question, one of the interviewers yells, "The hammer on your partner's gun is slowly moving back! What are you going to do?"

The worst thing you can do is not answer the question. At this point, you already have an answer, or you don't have a clue. Stop reading now, and write down what you believe to be the best answer.

Then write down any other possible answers you can think of. Take as much time as you need.

Officer talks to a group of people on the street

Subject under the influence of a controlled substance responds violently and is subsequently subdued with a tazer gun and hobbles

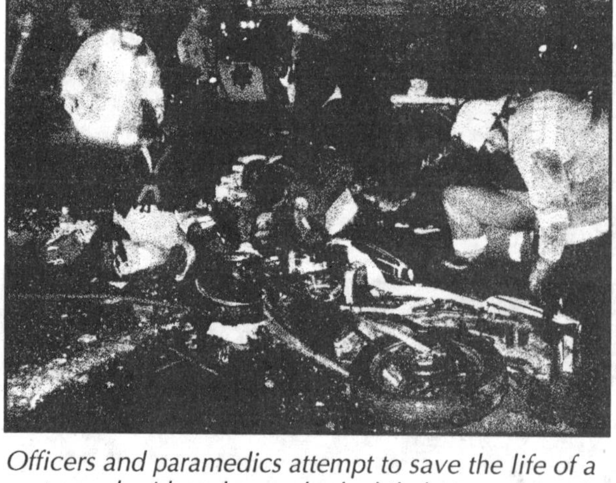

Officers and paramedics attempt to save the life of a motorcycle rider who crashed while being pursued by police at speeds in excess of 90 mph

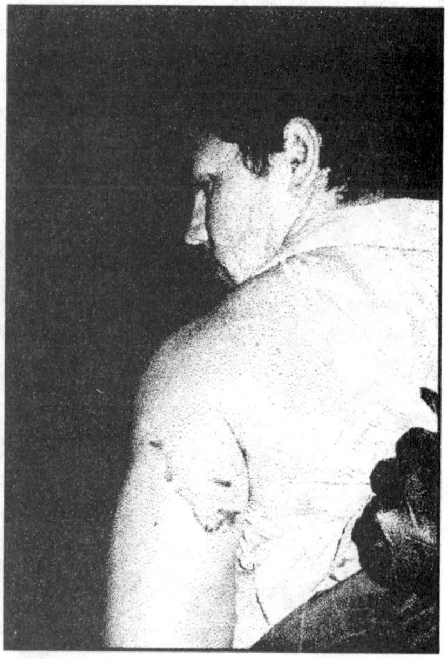

Following a routine domestic violence call, the suspect attempts to run from the police. He was subsequentlly caught and bitten by a Police K-9 dog. Note the torn shirt and bite marks.

Officer prepares for a physical encounter with a walk-away mental patient

Photographs courtesy of Robert J. Piel

Officers respond to a call about a man under the influence of PCP. To subdue him, he was shot with a tazer gun and lies dazed in the street.

A Police Sergeant talks with a biker following a bar fight

Figure 4-9: *What appears to be a routine call may suddenly escalate into a crisis situation*

Now we will go over the possible answers to this question, and you can compare our answers to your written answers. The first thing to keep in mind is that, unless your answer is completely bizarre, it will probably be accepted by your interviewers. This also applies to most of the other similar questions you may receive during the interview. Our answers are in the order that we feel is the best direct reaction to this situation.

deadly force: overcoming a suspect by attempting to kill him or her

1. If you are convinced your partner's life is in danger, quickly draw your weapon (if it's not already drawn), and take the best available shot. Most often this will be the head. Keep in mind that **deadly force** can be used only if you are convinced, beyond any doubt, that your partner will die if you do not shoot. If you are not positive the interviewer has described a **life or death** situation in the particular scenario, do not resort to deadly force.

   Attempt to create a diversion to allow your partner to initiate a defensive action. For example, begin moving in a peculiar manner or walking to the blind side of the offender to draw his attention for a split second.

2. Try to calm the offender by talking to him in a polite manner.

3. Quickly retreat to a location where you can get assistance, but do not leave your partner if possible.

Regardless of your answer, the important fact is that you are capable of making a reasonable decision. Although the answers may seem harsh, consider the scenario. Pursuing a career in law enforcement can often force you into these harsh positions.

After you have committed to a course of action, back it up by saying that you are sure with the proper training, you will respond in an appropriate manner.

When you are asked a question, do not immediately respond with your rehearsed answer. Pause for fifteen to twenty seconds, and apply your answer to the things we have discussed. We cannot give you every hypothetical question you may be asked, but we can provide you with a style or formula that will allow you to use common sense and provide an appropriate answer.

Most of the hypothetical questions you will be asked have arisen from real situations. Many of the real situations transpired in a period of no more than five or ten seconds, and an officer was forced to make a split-second decision. If you *freeze up* during this period of pressured decision making, your inability to make a decision will cost you a passing score.

> **This is the purpose of a stress interview — to see how you respond under pressure.**

Not every person can handle the severe stress and pressure of making difficult decisions day in and day out. Stress interviews are crucial in assuring the public their protectors are both physically and mentally equipped to protect them. However, it is important for you to understand that training and experience will increase your ability to make sound decisions under pressure.

During the stress interview, the interviewers are merely looking at your ability to reason and react. This backs up our belief that any answer is far better than no answer at all.

Figure 4-10: *Watch police television shows to help you learn discretionary decision making*

In your spare time, watch several different types of police television shows, and pay close attention to the decisions the officers make. Ask yourself how you would react. If you are preparing for an oral interview, this is the most accessible tutor you can find when it comes to discretionary decision making. Not only are these shows fun to watch, but with the right frame of mind, you can learn an amazing amount of information. Just remember not to cite your avid viewing of ***Cops*** as a motivator in the pursuit of your career.

Summary

In this chapter, you learned what to expect during the oral interview. You were introduced to the nonstress interview and the stress interview. Although you were not given all of the questions you can expect to be asked, you were given a sampling of the types of questions that will be asked and taught how to respond. You also learned how to apply common sense when giving your answers to the interview board.

Learning Activities

Discussion Question

Scan your TV Viewing Guide and pick three police dramas to watch. Write down each incident in which an officer must make a decision and the officer's decision. Note whether it was a pressured decision or simply a decision that had to be made. Be prepared to discuss these decisions with the class. Compare the types of decisions that were made by the officers in each program. Do you see any pattern to the decisions?

True/False Questions

T F 1. The oral interview is a test designed to check your ability to verbalize your thoughts and react under pressure.

T F 2. Writing an autobiography wIll help you prepare for the interview.

T F 3. It will not help you to practice speaking in front of a make-believe oral interview board.

T F 4. You should wear casual clothes that are loose and comfortable, such as jeans and a T-shirt to the oral interview.

T F 5. You should not chew gum or suck on mints during the interview.

T F 6. Drinking a lot of coffee before the interview will help you answer the questions faster.

T F 7. Being brief and honest with your answers after taking a few seconds to think about the question is better than giving a long, drawn-out answer that really does not answer the question.

T F 8. You should take the time to learn about the demography of the area that you have applied to work in before the oral interview.

T F 9. If you think the interviewers do not like your answer, you should immediately change it.

T F 10. The oral interview may last an hour or more.

Chapter Five
The Medical Examination

Objectives

When you have completed this chapter, you will understand:

1. What you should do to prepare for the physical examination
2. What type of clothing you should wear for the physical examination
3. The types of tests you will undergo during your physical examination
4. The purpose of each test you will undergo

Key Terms

- treadmill
- EKG (electrocardiogram)
- spirometer

Introduction

The medical examination that all applicants for a position in law enforcement undergo is basically a very thorough physical inspection of your body. The examination will be conducted by a licensed physician who practices in a private office or clinic. The agency that is processing your application will be required to pay for the physician's services as well as any other associated costs.

You should reserve a full day for this examination. You will be required to submit blood and urine samples for analysis. Among other things, the urinalysis will reveal the presence of illegal drugs. You may also have to perform a treadmill stress test. However, this test is not required by all agencies. On most occasions, you will be notified in advance if you must undergo testing on a treadmill.

The Treadmill Test

treadmill: a device activated by foot power or electronics that simulates walking or running to increase the heart rate

If you are notified that you will be given a **treadmill** test, take the following precautions prior to the test:

- Eat the same breakfast that was recommended in the chapter on physical agility testing unless you are otherwise instructed. If blood and urine testing are to be performed, you will probably be instructed not to eat for twelve hours before the test. However, you may drink water. Always follow the physician's directions, so that accurate results can be obtained.
- Do moderate stretching exercises just before the test. If you need to, ask the attending physician to allow time for you to loosen up before the test. You do not want to take the chance of getting injured this far along in the process.

- Wear loose-fitting clothing such as a sweatsuit, or wear shorts and a T-shirt under your outer clothing.

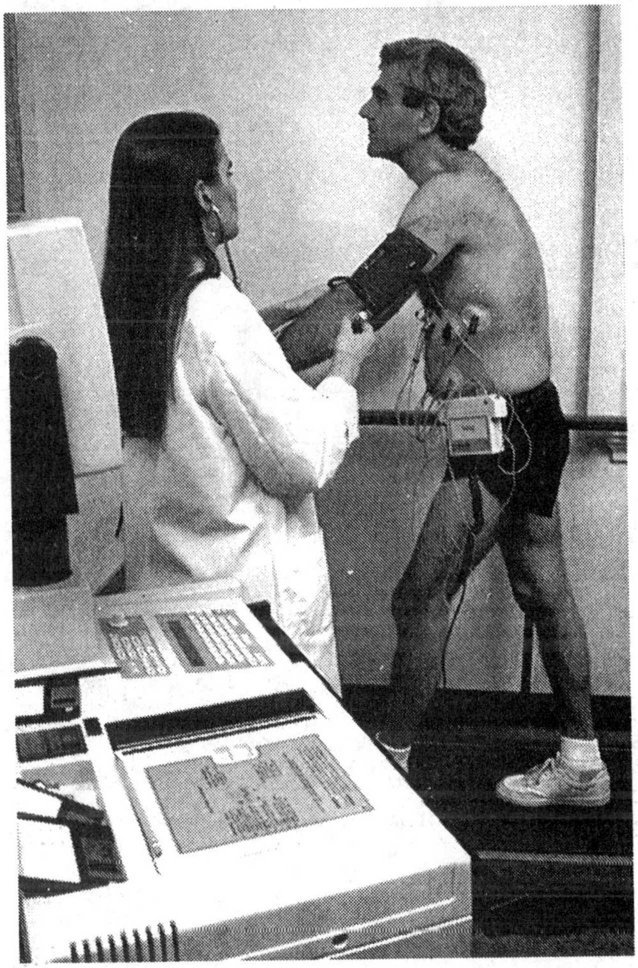

Figure 5-1: *Man undergoing a treadmill test*

The treadmill test is designed to raise your heart rate to a maximum peak of beats per minute. Then it will sustain your peak heart rate for a period of time. As the test concludes, your heart rate will slowly return back to its normal beat. Before, during, and after the test, your heart's rhythm will be recorded on an **EKG (electrocardiogram)**.

EKG (electrocardiogram): a tracing made by an electrocardiograph while measuring your heart action

The purpose of the EKG is to assure the testers that your heart is responding correctly under physical stress. In most cases, the test will take approximately thirty minutes and there are rarely any complications. If you should show any signs of abnormal stress, the test will be stopped immediately, so that you will not be endangered.

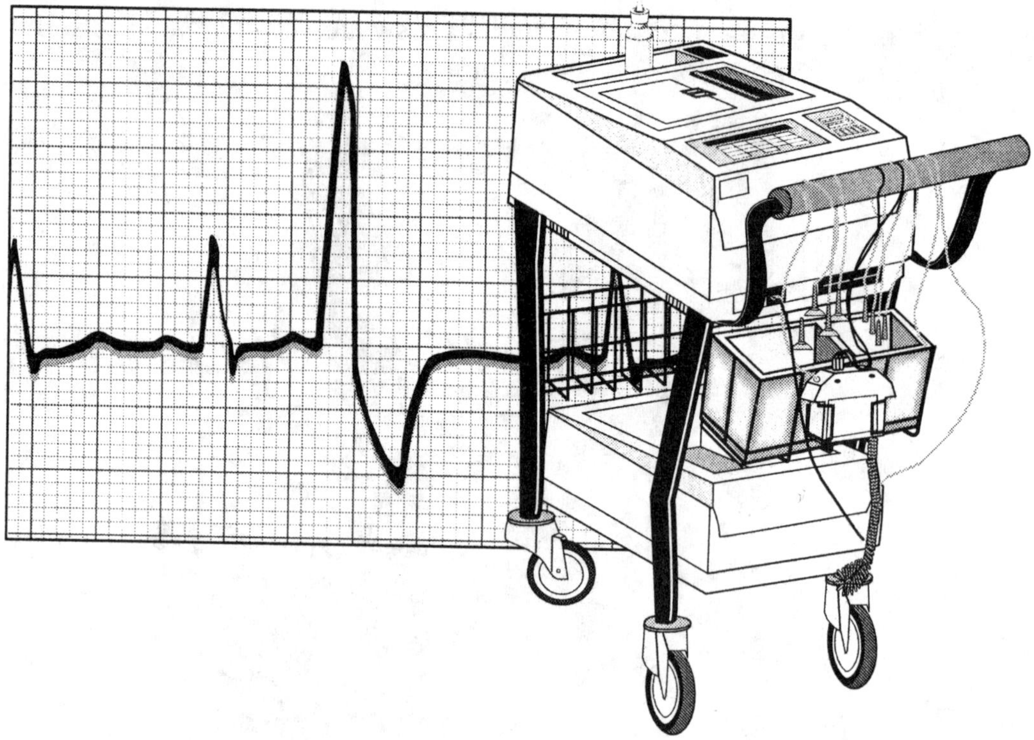

Figure 5-2: *Electrocardiograph and the tracing made on an electrocardiogram*

To briefly sum up the procedure, you are going to run on a rotating track for about twenty minutes. If you have already passed the physical agility test, then this test should be fairly easy.

Vision Testing

For obvious reasons, good vision is very important to law enforcement personnel. Many applicants are affected by the strict requirements regarding eyesight. Even though you may have poor eyesight, most agencies will accept those applicants that have acceptable corrected vision. Generally, if your eyesight is 20/100 or better and correctable to 20/20, you are considered acceptable. However, some agencies have their own specialized requirements.

If your vision is not 20/20 without correction, the most important thing to remember is that you should inform the recruiter before participating in the hiring process. Do not expect the agency to ask you about your vision. In almost all cases, they will not ask.

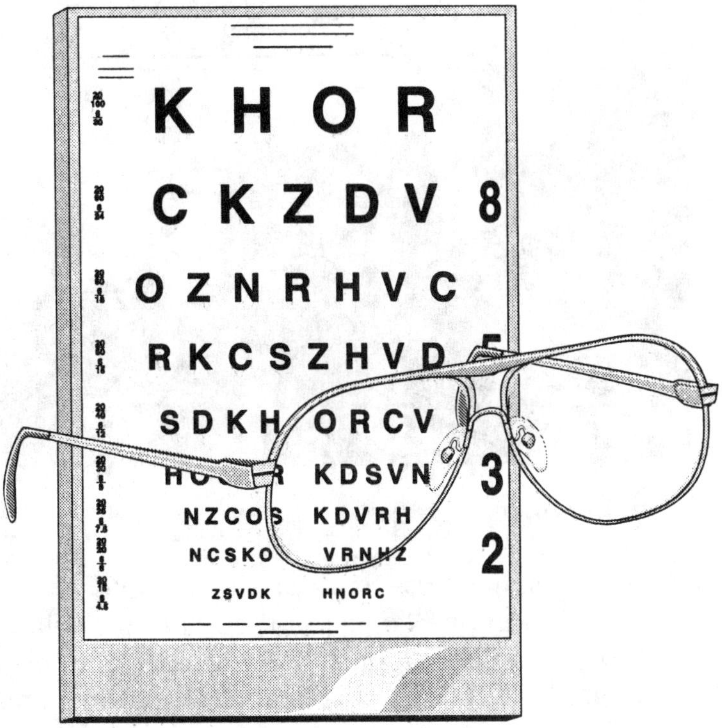

Figure 5-3: *Eyechart used to test vision*

If your vision is worse than 20/100, do not think you cannot find a place in law enforcement. There are agencies that will accept poor vision without limitation as long as it can be corrected with eyeglasses or contact lenses. Another alternative to keep in mind is that in some cases poor eyesight can be corrected by surgery. Ask a specialist about this option before you give up.

The Spirometer

The **spirometer** is an instrument that is designed to test and record your lung capacity. It measures the amount of inhaled and exhaled air and records it on a spirogram. It can then determine your maximum oxygen intake.

spirometer: an instrument that measures lung capacity

Figure 5-4: *The spirometer tests lung capacity*

Law enforcement personnel use it primarily to detect asthma or other abnormal breathing conditions. For certain positions in the law enforcement community, the officer must not be subject to attacks of asthma or suffer from other breathing difficulties. This is an optional test and may not be required by your potential employer.

The lung test is performed by inhaling and exhaling while blowing into a tube that passes through a computer. The only advice we can offer on preparing for this test is:

- Do not expose yourself to any unhealthful air conditions for at least 36 hours prior to the test. That means you should avoid physical activity if you live in an area that has a smog problem or work in an area with unhealthful breathing conditions.

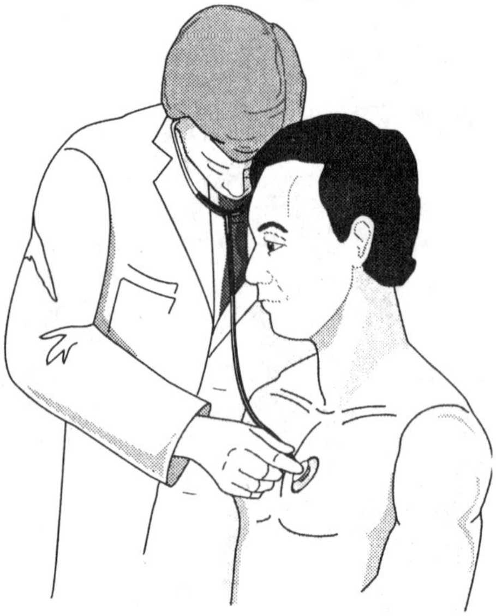

Figure 5-5: *Examination by a physician*

Concluding the Physical Exam

The physical testing will conclude with a brief examination of your body by a doctor. You will not know the results of the physical examination until your prospective employer receives a detailed report from the examining physician. This report will take anywhere from one to four weeks.

Summary

In this chapter, you learned what to do to prepare for the physical examination, the types of tests you will undergo, as well as the purpose of each test. You also learned about the necessity of having good vision and unimpaired breathing. Finally, you learned who will receive the results of the physical examination.

Learning Activities

True/False Questions

Instructions: Circle the T if the statement is true, or circle the F if the statement is false.

T F 1. The agency requesting the medical examination will pay for the exam.

T F 2. You do not have to submit to blood and urine testing unless you wish to.

T F 3. The treadmill test will determine your ability to lift heavy objects.

T F 4. You should wear loose clothing such as a warm-up suit or sweatsuit for the examination.

T F 5. Your eyesight will not matter much in determining whether you qualify as an applicant for a job in law enforcement.

T F 6. The treadmill test is simply to test your heart action.

T F 7. The spirometer is designed to test your body fat.

T F 8. You should check the eyesight requirements of the agency to which you have applied if you know you have impaired vision.

T F 9. One hour should be reserved for the physical examination.

T F 10. Among other things, the urine test tells whether you have used illegal drugs.

Chapter Six
The Polygraph

Objectives

When you have completed this chapter, you will understand:

1. How a polygraph functions
2. What type of testing the polygraph does
3. The types of questions you will be asked
4. The choices you will have in answering the questions
5. What you should avoid when being tested

Key Terms

- polygraph
- galvanometer
- blood pressure cuff
- countermeasure

Introduction

For most people, the thought of taking a polygraph, or lie detector, test strikes instant fear in their hearts. Relax. We all have something in our pasts that we would not care to share with others. The chances are your worries are unfounded, and your secrets will not be revealed. A little understanding of the testing instrument should help ease your fears.

The Polygraph

polygraph: an instrument for receiving and recording simultaneously tracings of changes in various body activities

What is the polygraph and how does it work? The polygraph is an instrument that needs no electricity to operate. However, the small electric motor that moves the graph paper through the instrument requires the instrument to be plugged into a wall socket. You are in no danger of being shocked and the test will be completely painless.

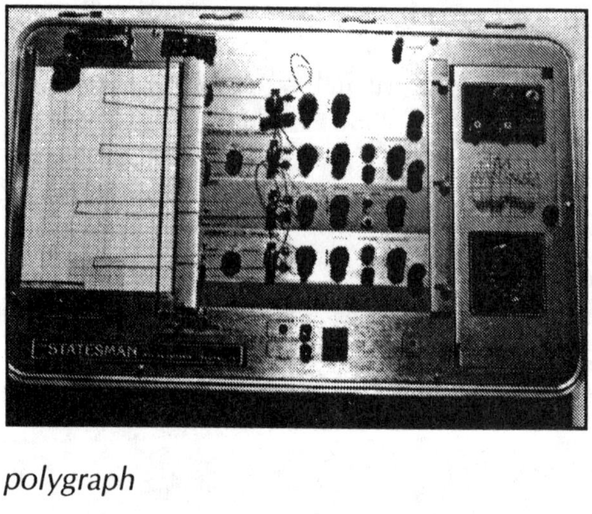

Photograph courtesy of Robert J. Piel

Figure 6-1: *The polygraph*

There are three main components that the examiner will attach to your body. The first component consists of two expanding and retracting spring-like devices that wrap around your upper and lower chest. These devices record the changes in your respiration, or breathing. They are called pneumos.

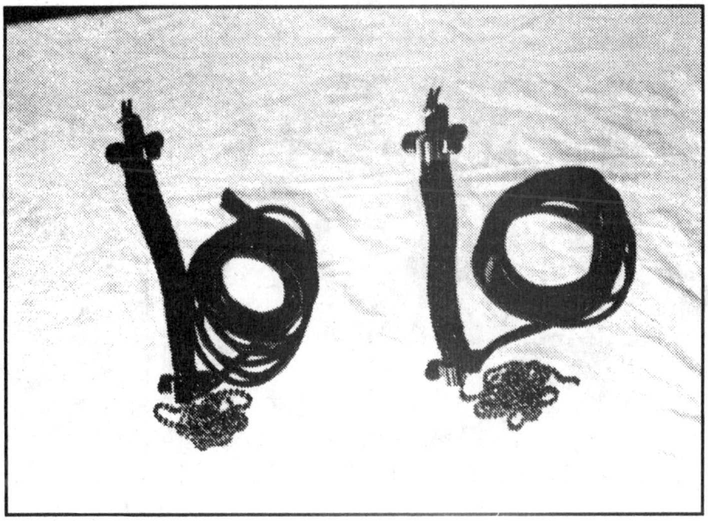

Photograph courtesy of Robert J. Piel

Figure 6-2: *The pneumo wraps around your chest and records changes in respiration*

The second component is called a **galvanometer**. Finger electrodes rest on your index and ring fingers and are held in place by Velcro straps. The other end of the electrode plugs into the galvanometer on the polygraph. The galvanometer then records the changes in the electrical resistance of your skin. These changes are called *electrodermal impulses.*

galvanometers: instruments that measure the electrical resistance of the skin

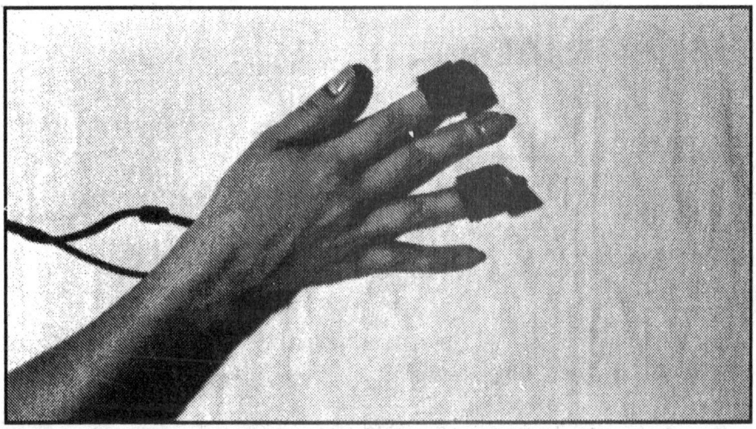

Photograph courtesy of Robert J. Piel

Figure 6-3: *Metal contacts are placed on the fingers to enable the recording of changes of the resistance of the examinee's skin*

blood pressure cuff: an instrument that records changes in blood pressure and pulse rate

The **blood pressure cuff** is the third component. It can be similar or identical to the standard blood pressure cuff used by the medical field. In some cases, the examiner may choose to use a plethysmograph or PLE finger clip in place of the blood pressure cuff. The clip is easier to use and is more comfortable for the examinee to wear. They both record blood pressure and pulse rate.

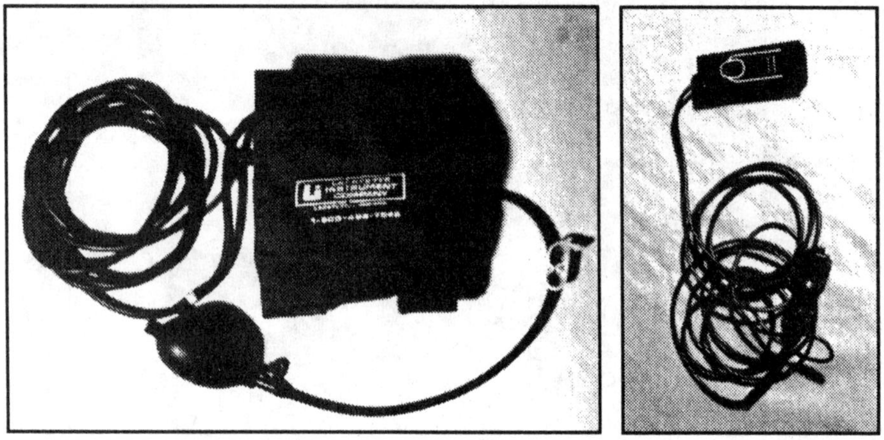

Photographs courtesy of Robert J. Piel

Figure 6-4: *A blood pressure cuff and a plethysmograph, or PLE finger clip*

The theory behind the polygraph examination is that the fear of detection will cause physiological changes to occur in a person's body when he or she tells a lie. Any changes in the body are recorded and then evaluated by a trained polygraph examiner. Because of the personal interpretation needed, the test is only as good as the examiner. However, in most cases, any examiner employed by a law enforcement agency will have a respectable record as a qualified expert.

Polygraph Testing

The polygraph has three major limitations.

1. It can only verify or discredit what the person *believes* to be true. It cannot verify or discredit actual fact.
2. It is a subjective diagnostic test, and its accuracy depends upon the ability and proficiency of the examiner.
3. Emotionally disturbed people can rarely be tested accurately because they often have a distorted perception of reality.

If you are worried about being called a liar when, in fact, you are being truthful, you really need not worry. The chances of this type of misinterpretation are extremely low. As a matter of fact, if the examiner is not absolutely positive you are lying, he will in all probability give you the benefit of the doubt.

If he is fairly sure you are lying, but the charts do not completely and overwhelmingly show your deception, the test will probably be called *inconclusive*. Then you will be retested. The second test may be done by the same examiner or by a different examiner and may occur on the same date or later. On some occasions, the person is simply passed and allowed to continue with the testing process.

Obviously, the decision will depend on the topic that is in question. If you have registered a possible deception in an area regarding illegal narcotic sales or a violent felony, then it will be investigated further. If it is of a minor nature, it will probably be overlooked. The decision is left to the discretion of both the examiner and the testing agency.

The best advice we can offer any applicant is, "Don't Lie!" If you tell the truth, you cannot help but pass. Think about this for a minute. The polygraph examination is designed to detect a lie as well as to detect truthfulness. When you tell the truth, you have two things working in your favor. The polygraph will not detect a lie, and it will detect you are telling the truth. If you are completely honest, how can you fail?

You may have heard your friends bragging about how they lied and *got away with it.* Although this is possible, it is highly unlikely. It is more plausible that the lies were not considered as significant as the person thought they were. You should also keep in mind the examiner is trained and probably knows something about the theory of polygraph testing that the average person will never know.

Regardless, if you try to conceal something that happened in your past, you will fail. Let your potential employer decide if the information you disclose is of a disqualifying nature. The acknowledgment of your mistakes and your willingness to accept responsibility shows integrity. If you are willing to lie, that indicates you cannot be trusted. Which person would you rather hire?

The majority of applicants with whom I have dealt have experimented with illegal drugs in the past. Today, most agencies will accept experimental drug use in the past as long as a reasonable period of time has elapsed since the applicant last used them. A period of three to five years is usually considered a reasonable period of time. You must decide if your use was experimental or if it went beyond that.

They will not hire an applicant, however, who has sold illegal narcotics, been addicted to drugs or treated for drug addiction, or who has been convicted of a felony regarding any drug involvement.

If you have used drugs in the past, be prepared to discuss this prior use with the examiner. However, do not offer the information unless it is requested. If the examiner does inquire about past drug use, simply explain what you did and how long ago it was that you did it.

countermeasure: a deliberate act or movement performed at the time a question is asked that is an attempt to alter the polygraph recordings.

One of the most common mistakes applicants make during the polygraph examination is referred to as a **countermeasure**. This normally occurs at the point when an applicant is asked a question that they would prefer not to answer honestly. At that time, the applicant attempts to alter the polygraph charts by deliberately moving a body part in a way that causes a response on the polygraph charts. It is amazing how many applicants ruin their test results by attempting this foolish act.

You cannot trick a competent examiner. Slowing your breathing, speeding it up, biting the inside of your cheek, putting a tack in your shoe and applying pressure with your toe, pinching your leg, etc., will not work, and will only cause you to fail the test.

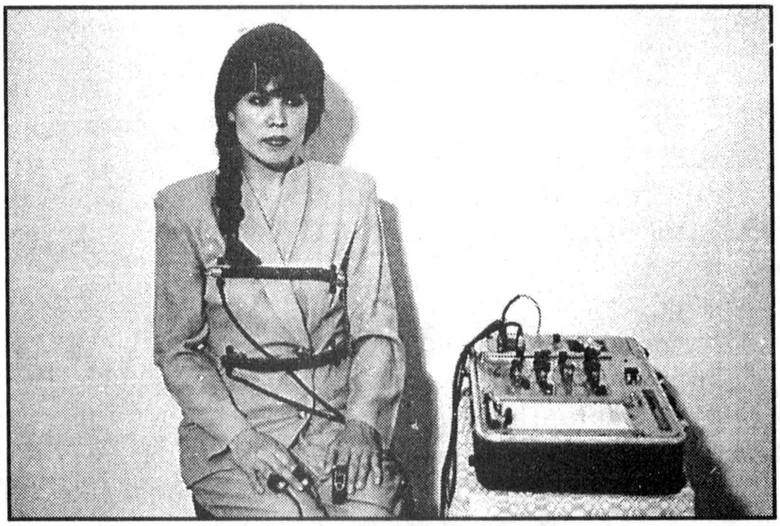

Photograph courtesy of Robert J. Piel

Figure 6-5: *Woman undergoing polygraph testing*

Now that you understand a little bit about the instrument used, we will discuss some of the more common questions you will be asked and how the testing process will be conducted. The best way to prepare for the test is not to prepare. That means you should not fill your days and spend sleepless nights worrying about all the minor illegal acts you have committed throughout your life.

Suppose the examiner asks you:

> *"Have you ever stolen anything from an employer?"*

If you are like most people you have. Assuming they were small items, such as pens, pencils, paper clips, etc., it would be all right to tell the examiner about that. It will not disqualify you. The examiner will then very likely rephrase the question and ask it in another way.

> *"Other than what you told me, have you ever stolen anything of great value from an employer?"*

By the way, you can count on seeing this question again.

If you have stolen valuable property from someone in the last five years, you had better have a good reason. Otherwise, we suggest you tell your potential employer about the incident before you take this test. Let them decide whether it is all right for you to go ahead with the polygraph test. Otherwise you would be better off to withdraw and let a little more time pass before you reapply.

The following are a few questions you will most likely be asked during the polygraph examination:

> *Regarding your application with our police department, do you have any reason to be concerned about an investigation into your work record?*
>
> *What about your military record?*
>
> *Do you have an undisclosed arrest record?*
>
> *Are you physically fit?*
>
> *Have you used illegal drugs within the last three years?*

As you can see, the questions are general and do not pry too deeply into your personal life.

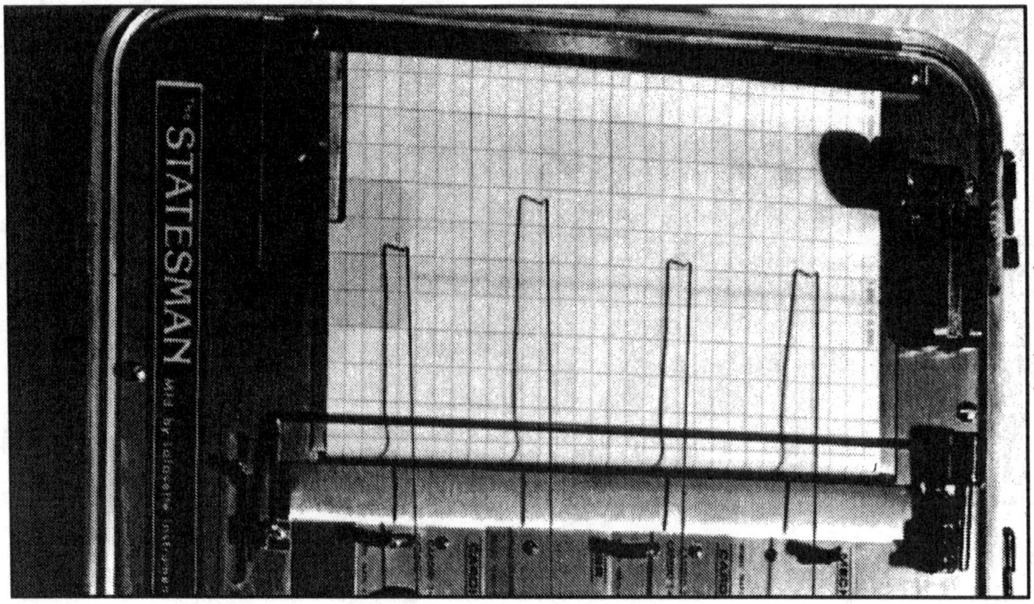

Photograph courtesy of Robert J. Piel

Figure 6-6: *The area of the polygraph where the charts are made*

The examiner should run three tracings, or charts. This means that you will be asked the same set of questions four times: once before the actual test, and three times during the test. The questions will require a yes or no answer.

Asking the same questions more than one time is a normal procedure and is done for comparison purposes. It will provide you with the benefit of a doubt if any of your answers should prove inconclusive. If you need to explain any answers, tell the examiner during the pretest portion of the examination. He will simply modify the question to meet your satisfaction.

Following the polygraph testing, either you will be allowed to continue the application process and proceed to the psychological testing portion, or you will be disqualified for having lied. If you are sincere about obtaining a job in law enforcement, I cannot emphasize too strongly:

Do not lie while taking your polygraph test.

Summary

In this chapter, you learned how a polygraph functions and what type of testing it does. You also learned about the types of questions you will be asked and the choice of answers you will have. You also discovered there are certain things you should never do while being tested.

Learning Activities

True/False Questions

Instructions: Circle the T if the statement is true, or circle the F if the statement is false.

T F 1. The polygraph will deliver a slight shock if you lie.

T F 2. If the examiner is not positive you are lying, he will give you the benefit of the doubt and pass you or test you again.

T F 3. Changing your normal breathing patterns during the test will fool the examiner if you lie.

T F 4. There is really no way to prepare for this test, other than resolve to tell the truth.

T F 5. The examiner will ask lots of very personal questions about your entire life.

T F 6. The polygraph monitors and records your breathing, blood pressure, electrical skin resistance, and pulse rate.

T F 7. Telling the truth is the best way to pass the polygraph test.

T F 8. If you have stolen a pen or other small item from a previous employer, you will very likely be disqualified from the testing process.

T F 9. If you have done something you believe may disqualify you, you should tell the recruiter before any testing and then let them decide whether you can continue in the testing process.

T F 10. A minor problem may not automatically disqualify you if you are honest.

Chapter Seven

The Psychological Examination

Objectives

When you have completed this chapter, you will understand:

1. Why a complete psychological examination is necessary for applicants in law enforcement fields
2. The two separate testing procedures that are administered
3. What the MMPI measures and its limitations
4. What the applicant should do to prepare for the testing
5. Aspects of the test itself that require caution

Key Terms

- MMPI
- liability
- profile

Introduction

profile: set of predetermined attributes that characterize a certain type of person

Most agencies require their applicants to be psychologically evaluated. The evaluation will be conducted by a licensed clinical psychologist or psychiatrist. Once again, this will most likely be an all day event, so come prepared. Get plenty of rest and eat a good breakfast.

The purpose of this test is to assure that you *psychologically* fit the **profile** of a *normal* law enforcement officer, and the primary reason for the evaluation is something that you will hear quite often in law enforcement — liability. What do we mean by the word liability?

Profile of a Normal Law Enforcement Officer

Trustworthy
Honest
Uses Sound Judgment
Has Good Sense
No Substance Abuse

Mentally Stable
Reliable
Calm in Emergencies
Ethical
Maintains Self-control

Liability

liability: being responsible for injury to another person or their property by failing to act or overreacting to a situation

In simple terms, liability means failing to act or overreacting in any situation that does — or could — result in injury to another person or their property. In the case of law enforcement agencies, they have the responsibility of assuring the public that every officer they employ is emotionally stable. If the agency fails to make an attempt to determine the state of an officer's psychological character before handing him or her a gun and sending them out on the streets, the agency could be found liable for failing to screen prospective employees properly if the officer loses control emotionally and injures someone.

An example of this type of behavior is an officer patrolling in a police vehicle who begins to have delusions of people shooting at him or her, and in fear for his or her life, stops the patrol car and shoots an innocent citizen. In all probability, the agency would be sued. If the officer had been properly tested psychologically before being hired, the agency would have a defense in court. They could have an expert testify the officer was psychologically evaluated and cleared to work as a police officer. This defense then helps reduce or eliminate the agency's liability, or responsibility, for the incident.

Many law enforcement agencies contract with private companies to administer the psychological testing. In addition to screening prospective employees for mental soundness, some agencies also have a description of what type of personalities *fit in best* with the character of their department and city. They will then ask the examiners to eliminate the people who do not fit that particular profile.

There is a very good reason for this procedure. It is an effort to ensure that any new employees will fit in with those already working for the agency. This attempt helps employees to sustain longer careers with the agency than those who do not mesh well with one another or the location.

This type of screening is a very good reason **not** to be discouraged if you do not pass this phase of testing for a particular agency. I was recently told by a chief of police, "If an applicant does not fit our profile, he or she may be a perfect fit for the neighboring city."

The Testing Procedure

The psychological evaluation will be split into two parts: the written test and the oral interview. Do not confuse this interview with the oral interview in Chapter Three. They are quite different and serve different purposes. We will start with the written test.

The Written Test

MMPI: Minnesota Multiphasic Personality Inventory

The written test is known as the MMPI-II. (Minnesota Multiphasic Personality Inventory, Version II). The MMPI was originally developed at the University of Minnesota in 1942. It is a very complex test with 567 true/false questions. Although the questions are simple, taking the test is a long, tiresome process that can last several hours.

Figure 7-1: *Applicant taking the written test*

How was the test created and what is it designed to do? Several researchers from the University of Minnesota formulated 567 questions structured to reveal different personality traits. In simple-to-understand terms, the questions were given to various mentally disturbed persons. The questions were also given to a group of *normal* people who were referred to as the *Minnesota Normals.* The answers were then studied and compared to determine what separated *normal* from *abnormal.* Over the years, society's morals and values have changed. In 1989, the test was revised to reflect the most recent changes.

The test was designed to be used as an evaluating tool only and should never be considered as absolute confirmation that a person is either psychologically normal or abnormal. That is why your written test will be followed by a personal interview with the psychologist.

Through research, it has been discovered that this testing is valuable only if the psychologist who is administering the examination is completely competent. There is a great deal of room for misjudgment, so don't panic if you fail.

During the writing of this book, we discovered that applicants often both pass and fail this area of testing when they apply to multiple agencies. It is quite possible that you can fail this test on one day and pass it the next. The psychologist we interviewed stated that this test was not a *pass/fail* test; however, if it is determined you do not fit the psychological profile of a law enforcement person and you are dropped from the testing process, then you obviously failed.

Limitations of the MMPI-II

The biggest problem with this test is that if the test subject is a good liar, it is difficult to detect mental impairment. The test relies on an honest examinee, and most criminals, as we know, tend to be dishonest. An inexperienced psychologist can easily err in determining your profile.

The authors have determined the area that is most likely to cause you to fail this portion of the hiring process relies on how you present yourself to the psychologist. Here are some tips on how to prepare.

- Make sure you have a complete night's sleep before the test (8 to 10 hours). If you are tired when you take the test and skip an answer or accidentally mark the wrong answer on a few questions, it can cost you a career. The written test requires **total concentration.**
- Eat a very nutritious meal prior to the test. If your stomach is growling and you are thinking about Big Macs, then you are not concentrating on the test.
- Allow yourself the entire day to complete this phase of testing. Do not plan to leave at a certain time or be somewhere else later. Have nothing else on your schedule for this day. For the entire day, the only thing on your mind should be this testing.

Before you begin answering the questions, read the instructions carefully. There are detailed directions on the inside cover of the test booklet. Take them seriously. You should apply all the questions to yourself. As the booklet indicates, answer the questions based on *Your own opinion of yourself.*

This test is not in the same format as the normal True/False Scantron type tests. Your answers to the questions will range from true to mostly true, false, and mostly false. However, you will have a choice of only true or false on the answer form. To determine whether you should answer a question true or false, break it down to a scale of 1 to 10. If the question is mostly true — meaning it rates a 6 or better — then answer it as true. Use the same decision determination pattern for a mostly false question.

Do not stop to mull over a question. If you hesitate over a difficult question, apply the decision formula, choose your answer, and move on to the next question.

Constantly check the Scantron answer form to make sure your answer number coincides with the number on the test booklet. If you are on answer number 344 on the answer form, make sure you are answering question number 344 in the booklet.

The questions on the test are very similar, so it is easy to skip some. Do not begin taking the test with the idea you can answer the questions in a manner that would make you appear perfect for the job. The test is composed of questions that the developers refer to as either *subtle or obvious.* They are designed to detect the person who is trying to appear *too normal.* Just be honest and careful as you answer the questions.

The following are sample questions that are similar to the questions you will encounter during the test. Remember, your answer may be true, mostly true, false, or mostly false, but you will have a choice of only true or false on the answer form.

1. *I enjoy reading computer magazines.*
2. *Sometimes I eat more than I should.*
3. *Demons live inside me.*
4. *Sometimes, I worry about dying.*
5. *I have trouble disposing of items I don't use.*
6. *After a long day, a few beers help me unwind.*
7. *I'm not afraid to die.*
8. *I feel safer in my home than I do outside.*
9. *I believe in ghosts.*
10. *I love animals.*

Before the Oral Interview

Before the oral interview, consider the possible questions you may be asked about coping with stress, changes in your lifestyle, conflicts with friends, family, and working erratic hours. The psychologist who interviews you will want to know how you think these things will affect your personal life, etc. Prepare mature answers to these questions. The more you prepare for answering these questions, the better the interview will proceed.

The Oral Interview

The oral interview with the psychologist will generally take place after you have taken the written test (MMPI). It is a relaxed interview that is almost conversational and lasts approximately thirty minutes. The psychologist will ask questions about you personally, your friends, and your family. He or she will ask how you cope with changes in your lifestyle and whether you think any of your friends will no longer want to associate with you because of your new career.

Photograph courtesy of Robert J. Piel

Figure 7-2: *Applicant and interviewer during the psychological oral interview*

You may also be asked about past experiences, and how you deal with stress and pressure. The interviewer may want to know what you think you would do if you were confronted with various situations. Some of these questions may be the same as those you answered on the MMPI test.

Try not to sound too eager as you reply. Think about your answer before you speak, and answer each question completely. If you sound evasive, the psychologist will be concerned about your character and motives for wanting a career in law enforcement. Keep the real reason why you want a career in law enforcement foremost in your mind. Do not let yourself be distracted from concentrating on this.

You will leave an impression with the psychologist, and you want this impression to be positive.

After the Test

Should you fail the evaluation, ask the psychologist what he or she felt was the problem or what you can do in the future to pass the test. If you pass and continue in the application process, the next step is the background investigation.

One Final Tip

One final tip on the psychological test. Stress is the largest career-destroying problem in law enforcement. Learning how to control and relieve it is something that every applicant should research and practice. There are many ways to handle stress, and it is very likely the psychologist will ask you how you handle yourself under pressure. As you think about this question, just keep in mind that any kind of physical activity such as bicycle riding, basketball, racquetball, etc., is an excellent answer to helping you relieve the stress that is most certainly a part of any job in law enforcement.

Summary

In this chapter, you learned the type of psychological testing that you will have to undergo. The written test (MMPI) was explained showing you how this test differs from a normal true/false test. The types of questions were discussed and the reasons you must use extreme care when taking the test. You also learned the oral examination is a relaxed, conversational type of test that lasts approximately thirty minutes. You were advised of the best ways to answer the interviewer's questions. Finally, you were reminded to always keep uppermost in your mind the primary reason you want to have a career in law enforcement.

Learning Activities

True/False Questions

T F 1. If you fail this exam, you could be admitted to a mental hospital.

T F 2. This portion of the hiring process will take most of the day to complete.

T F 3. This evaluation is designed to examine your personality traits.

T F 4. You may fail this part of the testing for one agency, but pass it the next day for a different agency.

T F 5. The most common test used is called the MMPI-II (Minnesota Multiphasic Personality Inventory.)

T F 6. None of the questions on this test are similar.

T F 7. Because of the large number of questions on this test, the applicant should frequently check to make sure he or she did not skip one because skipping one could ruin the entire test.

T F 8. All of the questions require true, mostly true, false, or mostly false answers.

T F 9. You should answer the questions in a way that makes you appear perfect for the job.

T F 10. Reading the directions on the test booklet will not help you pass the test.

Chapter Eight

The Background Investigation

Objectives

When you have completed this chapter, you will understand:

1. Why a background investigation is necessary
2. What information you must be sure to include when completing your background papers
3. Who will be contacted by the background investigator
4. What you can expect during the interviews with those persons you have given as personal references

Key Term

- FI (field interview)

Introduction

The background investigation is the final phase of your application process. You must pass this portion successfully in order to be hired for any position with a law enforcement agency. Even if you have passed all other phases of the testing, if your background investigation reveals anything that can disqualify you, you will not be hired. Again, the word liability plays a significant role. Agencies cannot risk hiring a person who does not meet the stringent requirements for their personal lives. They are placing their officers in a position of trust by the public, and these officers must be worthy of this trust.

What is the Background Investigation?

The background investigation is a complete and thorough check into your personal history. The background investigator's job is to contact anyone who can give him or her information regarding your past behavior.

In most cases, the investigation into your background will begin following the successful completion of the oral board interview. You will be given an extremely thick packet of papers with instructions to complete them by answering all of the questions and filling in the blanks. At this time, you will also be advised of the date when you will meet with the background investigator.

Preparing Background Papers

The following are some extremely important tips to remember when you are preparing your background papers and meeting with the investigator.

- Make a complete set of photocopies of the background papers after they are completed.

Photograph courtesy of Robert J. Piel

Figure 8-1: *Applicant receiving background papers to be completed*

- Inform your family, friends, employers, and neighbors that you have applied for employment with a particular agency, and a background investigator will probably contact them as character references.
- Do not list any person with whom you have ever had a serious falling-out as a character reference.
- Provide your background investigator with certified copies of your high school and college transcripts.
- Provide your military discharge documents if you have served in the armed forces.
- If you are married or divorced, a copy of these documents will be required.

The best way to avoid any problems in a background investigation is to have all your information ready and available for the investigator.

To elaborate on the points previously made, you should make copies of all the papers you complete and documents you submit. If you become involved in the hiring process with more than one agency, having those copies will save you hours of work.

Figure 8-2: *Applicant carefully completing background papers*

More importantly, the papers you submit become the property of the agency to which you have submitted them. Any other agency to which you apply in the future can request to examine those papers. They will compare the content of those papers with the ones you submit to them. If you have omitted any information or changed any of your answers to the specific questions, you will be disqualified.

Fill out your papers completely and accurately the first time, and never complete any other background papers without using the copies of the first papers as a guide.

The first thing the investigator will tell a character reference is that any information they provide will be in strict confidence. This advice is provided to motivate the reference to disclose everything about a person — including uncomplimentary facts. Therefore, even if you think a person with whom you have had a falling out is now your friend, any resentment toward you or your success may inspire him or her to provide negative information if they are listed as a character reference.

You should provide as much documentation for your life as you can — marriage license, divorce papers, discharge papers, educational diplomas, etc. The bottom line is that the background investigator's job requires an enormous amount of footwork. When you provide him or her with these types of documents, that means they will have to do less work on your investigation. They will appreciate your willingness to cooperate. Need we say more?

Providing these documents will not only save them time but will also show your willingness to be hired by their agency. If you are aware of a problem in your background that you have not disclosed, you can tell the investigator about the problem during a private interview.

Stop reading for a moment and ask yourself if there is anything in your background that could disqualify you during a background investigation. If your answer is yes, then decide now if there is any possibility the investigator can find it.

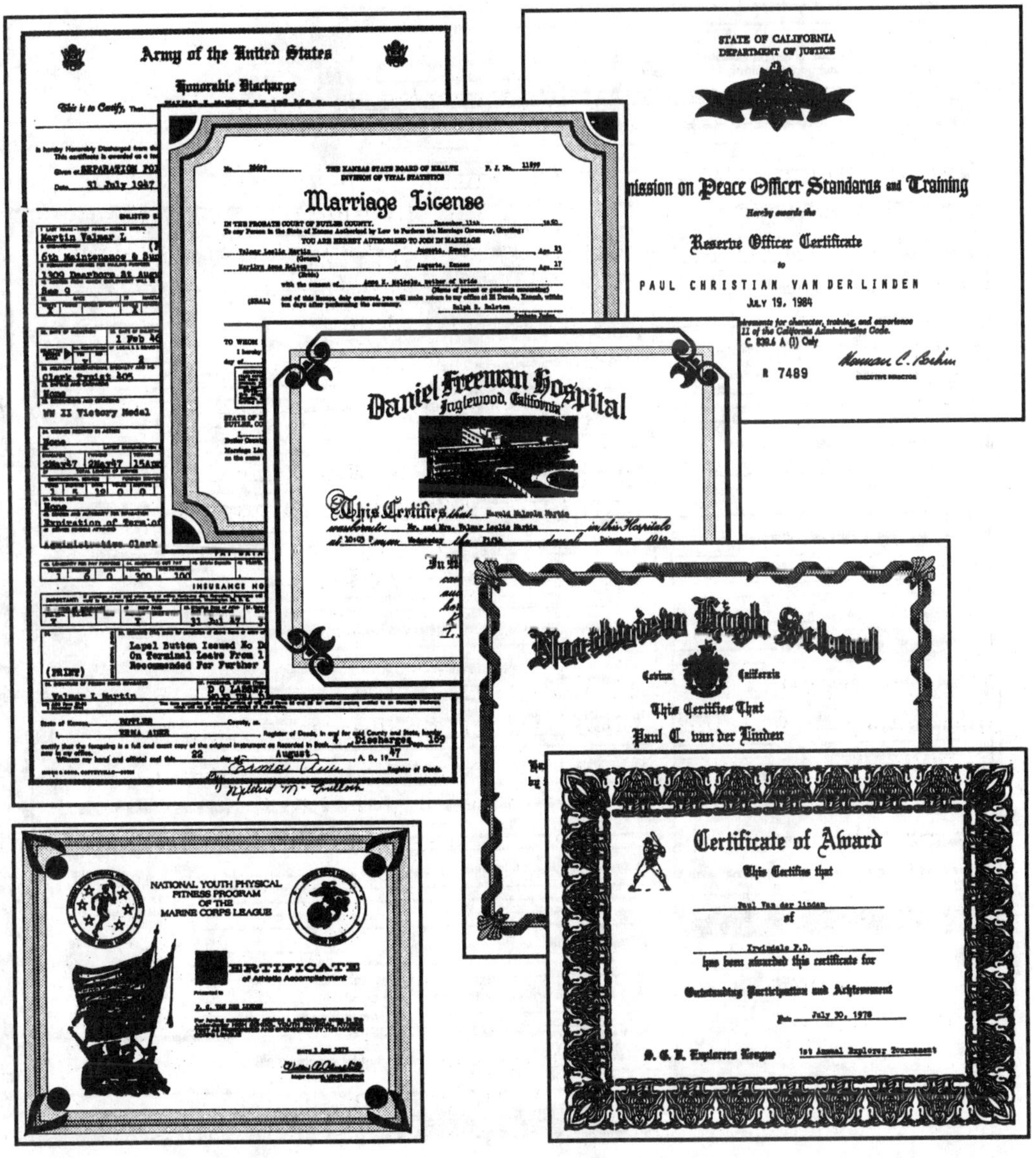

***Figure 8-3:** Documentation provided to support background investigation*

The Field Interviews

FI (field interview): a log kept by a police department on persons with whom officers have had contact

If you answered yes, you now know what information you must disclose. Keep this fact in mind. Local police departments keep what they call FIs (field interviews) on almost every person with whom the officers have had contact — no matter what the reason. The first thing the background investigator will do is contact the agencies in the areas where you have lived and inquire about any contacts they may have had with you.

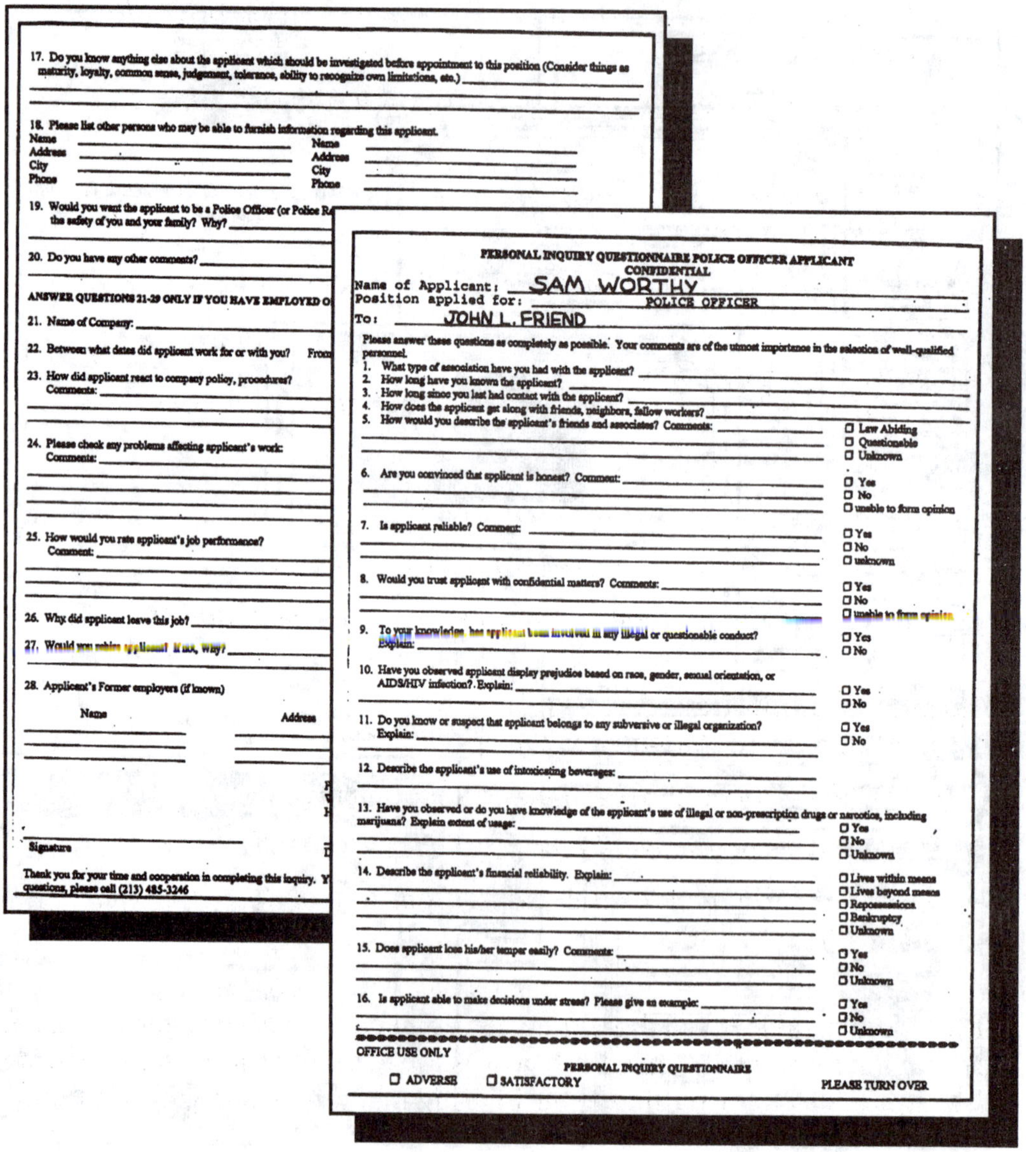

17. Do you know anything else about the applicant which should be investigated before appointment to this position (Consider things as maturity, loyalty, common sense, judgement, tolerance, ability to recognize own limitations, etc.)

18. Please list other persons who may be able to furnish information regarding this applicant.
Name / Address / City / Phone
Name / Address / City / Phone

19. Would you want the applicant to be a Police Officer (or Police R… the safety of you and your family? Why?

20. Do you have any other comments?

ANSWER QUESTIONS 21-29 ONLY IF YOU HAVE EMPLOYED O…

21. Name of Company:

22. Between what dates did applicant work for or with you? From

23. How did applicant react to company policy, procedures?
Comments:

24. Please check any problems affecting applicant's work:
Comments:

25. How would you rate applicant's job performance?
Comment:

26. Why did applicant leave this job?

27. Would you rehire applicant? If not, Why?

28. Applicant's Former employers (if known)
Name Address

Signature

Thank you for your time and cooperation in completing this inquiry. Y… questions, please call (213) 485-3246

PERSONAL INQUIRY QUESTIONNAIRE POLICE OFFICER APPLICANT
CONFIDENTIAL
Name of Applicant: SAM WORTHY
Position applied for: POLICE OFFICER
To: JOHN L. FRIEND

Please answer these questions as completely as possible. Your comments are of the utmost importance in the selection of well-qualified personnel.

1. What type of association have you had with the applicant?
2. How long have you known the applicant?
3. How long since you last had contact with the applicant?
4. How does the applicant get along with friends, neighbors, fellow workers?
5. How would you describe the applicant's friends and associates? Comments: ☐ Law Abiding ☐ Questionable ☐ Unknown
6. Are you convinced that applicant is honest? Comment: ☐ Yes ☐ No ☐ unable to form opinion
7. Is applicant reliable? Comment: ☐ Yes ☐ No ☐ unknown
8. Would you trust applicant with confidential matters? Comments: ☐ Yes ☐ No ☐ unable to form opinion
9. To your knowledge, has applicant been involved in any illegal or questionable conduct? Explain: ☐ Yes ☐ No
10. Have you observed applicant display prejudice based on race, gender, sexual orientation, or AIDS/HIV infection? Explain: ☐ Yes ☐ No
11. Do you know or suspect that applicant belongs to any subversive or illegal organization? Explain: ☐ Yes ☐ No
12. Describe the applicant's use of intoxicating beverages:
13. Have you observed or do you have knowledge of the applicant's use of illegal or non-prescription drugs or narcotics, including marijuana? Explain extent of usage: ☐ Yes ☐ No ☐ Unknown
14. Describe the applicant's financial reliability. Explain: ☐ Lives within means ☐ Lives beyond means ☐ Repossessions ☐ Bankruptcy ☐ Unknown
15. Does applicant lose his/her temper easily? Comments: ☐ Yes ☐ No ☐ Unknown
16. Is applicant able to make decisions under stress? Please give an example: ☐ Yes ☐ No ☐ Unknown

OFFICE USE ONLY
PERSONAL INQUIRY QUESTIONNAIRE
☐ ADVERSE ☐ SATISFACTORY
PLEASE TURN OVER

Figure 8-4: *Friends,acquaintances, former employers, etc., may receive a questionnaire similar to this one to complete*

Questioning Those Who Know You

After the agency receives the information from the police departments, the investigator will either mail questionnaires to people who know you or meet with them personally. The following are some questions they will be asked.

Friends, Family, Acquaintances

- *Do you know of any reason why we should not hire this person?*
- *Do you personally know if the applicant has ever used illegal narcotics?*
- *How does the applicant conduct himself or herself at social gatherings?*
- *Do you know of anyone else we may contact that may tell us more about the applicant?*
- *What type of drinking habits does the applicant have?*

Past and present employers

- *Why is the applicant no longer employed by your company?*
- *Is he or she eligible for rehire?*
- *Was the applicant a good employee?*
- *Was the applicant frequently late for work?*
- *Did he or she frequently call in sick? How many times?*

Educational institutions

- *What type of student was the applicant?*
- *Did the applicant participate in school activities?*
- *What type of grades did the applicant maintain?*
- *Was the applicant ever expelled from school. If so, for what reason?*

If you suspect that any of these questions will be answered negatively by any person the investigator may find, now is the time to sit down and document the explanations in writing. The investigator may want you to submit a written explanation.

Credit Report

It is also a common practice for background investigators to run a credit report on applicants. Therefore, you should make sure that all of your debt payments are current. If there is a problem with your past credit history, be prepared to explain the problem and the steps you have taken to solve it.

If you are currently involved in a bankruptcy and you are questioned about it, it would be better for you to withdraw from the application process until the matter is completely resolved through a bankruptcy court. After it has been resolved, then reapply with the agency.

Your Personal Interview

When you meet with the investigator, present the information in a professional manner along with your verbal explanation. If the investigator asks you to supply a written explanation, state that you have already completed it and hand it over.

The background investigation will take approximately four to six weeks to complete and is usually concluded at about the same time as the last phase of testing. If you supply the information as we have instructed, the process should move considerably faster.

At the conclusion of the investigation, the investigator will write a detailed report disclosing all of the positive and negative information he or she has discovered. The report will conclude with the investigator's recommendation that you should or should not be hired.

Summary

In this chapter, you learned what comprises the background investigation. You also learned who will be contacted and what type of documentation you should provide. Examples of questions that will be asked about you were provided. Finally, you learned what you should do in case you have negative events in your life that a background investigation will uncover.

Learning Activities

Carefully think back through your life. Write down anything you have done that you know was wrong. Then write down all incidents where you were blamed for something (whether or not you were to blame). Finally, write down everything you can think about your past actions that others will view negatively. These may include driving recklessly, losing your temper, cheating on a test, breaking promises, questionable ethical procedures, etc.

Place a check mark beside those of a serious enough nature to be brought up during the background investigation. Then write down your explanation for these actions. If you have improved or been trying to improve your performance in any of the areas, write down what you have done.

Now ask yourself this question.
Am I worthy of the public's trust?
If your answer is yes, write down why you think so.

Put each serious action and its explanation on a separate piece of paper. They should be typewritten if possible. These will now serve as your documentation during the background investigation when you are questioned about these events.

True/False Questions

T F 1. The background investigator will not verify anything I write on my background papers.

T F 2. Making a complete set of photocopies of the background papers after I fill them out will help me when I am applying to other agencies.

T F 3. Family, friends, and employers are seldom contacted by the investigator.

T F 4. If I do not tell the investigator about any bad things, he or she will not be able to find them out.

T F 5. If I have had a problem in my past, the best thing to do is explain it to the investigator before they find out.

T F 6. The background investigator will not be concerned about my school records.

T F 7. A written explanation about potential problems in my personal history will show a willingness to be honest.

T F 8. How I act at social gatherings and parties will not matter because everyone acts crazy when they are drunk.

T F 9. It is a good idea to let friends and family members know that an investigator may contact them regarding my personal history.

T F 10. The background investigator will not contact other law enforcement agencies in places where I used to live to see if they know me.

Background Papers

On the following pages is a set of real-life background papers. Complete the papers. Make a copy of the papers and hand them in to the instructor for his or her approval. Make any corrections he or she suggests, and save the papers for future use when applying to a law enforcement agency.

LATAH COUNTY SHERIFF'S OFFICE

BACKGROUND INFORMATION RECORD

POSITION: ( ) POLICE OFFICER/RECRUIT ( ) POLICE OFFICER/ LATERAL ENTRY

( ) COMMUNICATIONS SPECIALIST ( ) OTHER ______________________________

SECTION I - PERSONAL INFORMATION

FULL NAME: ______________________________

ALIASES, NICKNAMES, MAIDEN NAME: ______________________________

U.S. CITIZEN: ( ) yes ( ) no DATE OF BIRTH ______________

PLACE OF BIRTH: CITY______________ COUNTY ______________ STATE ______________

SEX ______ AGE ______ HEIGHT ______ WEIGHT ______ HAIR ______ EYES ______ SS# ______

DRIVERS LICENSE NO. ______________ STATE: ______ EXPIRES: ______

NAME OF AUTO INSURANCE COMPANY: ______________________________

HAVE YOU EVER BEEN TREATED FOR A NERVOUS OR MENTAL DISORDER? : ( ) YES ( ) NO

SECTION II - CURRENT RESIDENCE

ADDRESS: ______________________________

CITY: ______________ STATE: ______________ ZIP: ______________

PHONE: ( ) ______________ OWN ( ) RENT ( ) VISITING ( )

WITH WHOM DO YOU LIVE? ______________________________

RELATIONSHIP? ______________________________ LENGTH OF TIME: ______________

SECTION III - MARITAL INFORMATION

CHECK ONE OR MORE:	SINGLE ( )	MARRIED ( )	SEPARATED ( )
	DIVORCED ( )	WIDOWED ( )	REMARRIED ( )

SPOUSE'S NAME: ______________________________ MAIDEN NAME: ______________

AGE:______ DATE OF BIRTH: ______________ DATE OF MARRIAGE:______________

MARRIED AT: CITY: ______________ COUNTY: ______________ STATE: ______________

SPOUSE'S EMPLOYER: ______________________________ PHONE: ( ) ______________

EMPLOYER'S ADDRESS: ______________________________

SPOUSE'S POSITION OR TITLE: ______________________________

LENGTH OF TIME EMPLOYED: ______ YEARS ______ MONTHS SALARY ______________

LIST ALL YOUR CHILDREN, INCLUDING STEP CHILDREN ADOPTED CHILDREN, ETC.:

NAME	RELATIONSHIP	DATE OF BIRTH

OTHER CHILDREN MAY BE LISTED ON PAGE 15.

IF DIVORCED OR ANNULLED, LIST PRIOR MARRIAGES IN ORDER OF OCCURRENCE:

NAME OF FORMER SPOUSE ______________________

PRESENT ADDRESS OF FORMER SPOUSE ______________________

TELEPHONE NUMBER (   ) ____________ DATE DIVORCE FINAL ________

CITY ____________ COUNTY____________ STATE ____________

AMOUNT OF CHILD SUPPORT OR ALIMONY ORDERED $____________

HAVE YOU EVER BEEN DELINQUENT ON PAYMENTS? ( ) YES ( ) NO

IF YES, EXPLAIN ______________________

NAME OF FORMER SPOUSE ______________________

PRESENT ADDRESS OF FORMER SPOUSE ______________________

TELEPHONE NUMBER (   ) ____________ DATE DIVORCE FINAL ________

CITY ____________ COUNTY____________ STATE ____________

AMOUNT OF CHILD SUPPORT OR ALIMONY ORDERED $____________

HAVE YOU EVER BEEN DELINQUENT ON PAYMENTS? ( ) YES ( ) NO

IF YES, EXPLAIN ______________________

LIST THE DESCRIPTION OF ANY VEHICLES YOU OWN.

YEAR	MAKE	MODEL	COLOR	LICENSE #

SECTION IV - RESIDENCE INFORMATION

LIST ALL RESIDENCES FOR THE PAST 15 YEARS. BEGIN WITH CURRENT RESIDENCE.
SHOW THE COMPLETE ADDRESS ON THE TOP LINE IN EACH BLOCK AND SHOW WITH WHOM YOU'VE LIVED, INCLUDING NAME AND RELATIONSHIP, ON THE SECOND LINE.

FROM	TO	
FROM	TO	
FROM	TO	
FROM	TO	
FROM	TO	
FROM	TO	
FROM	TO	
FROM	TO	
FROM	TO	
FROM	TO	
FROM	TO	
FROM	TO	
FROM	TO	

SECTION V - FAMILY HISTORY

LIST RELATIVES IN THE FOLLOWING ORDER: MOTHER (MAIDEN NAME), STEP-MOTHER, FOSTER MOTHER, FATHER, STEP-FATHER, FOSTER FATHER, LEGAL GUARDIAN, BROTHERS, SISTERS, MOTHER-IN-LAW AND FATHER- IN- LAW.

EXAMPLE FORM TO FOLLOW: RELATIONSHIP, AGE, NAME (LAST, FIRST, MIDDLE), OTHER NAMES (NICKNAMES, MAIDEN NAME), ADDRESS (NUMBER, STREET, CITY, STATE, ZIP), BIRTHPLACE AND OCCUPATION.

ADDITIONAL FAMILY MEMBERS MAY BE LISTED ON PAGE 15.

SECTION VI - EMPLOYMENT INFORMATION

LIST ALL PERIODS OF EMPLOYMENT, UNEMPLOYMENT, SCHOOLS AND OTHER LAPSES IN TIME FOR THE PAST FIFTEEN (15) YEARS. BEGIN WITH YOUR PRESENT EMPLOYER.

EMPLOYER'S NAME ______________________ PHONE (___) ____________
ADDRESS ______________________________________
EMPLOYED FROM __________ TO __________
JOB TITLE ______________________________________
SALARY __________ REASON FOR LEAVING ______________________

EMPLOYER'S NAME ______________________ PHONE (___) ____________
ADDRESS ______________________________________
EMPLOYED FROM __________ TO __________
JOB TITLE ______________________________________
SALARY __________ REASON FOR LEAVING ______________________

EMPLOYER'S NAME ______________________ PHONE (___) ____________
ADDRESS ______________________________________
EMPLOYED FROM __________ TO __________
JOB TITLE ______________________________________
SALARY __________ REASON FOR LEAVING ______________________

EMPLOYER'S NAME ______________________ PHONE (___) ____________
ADDRESS ______________________________________
EMPLOYED FROM __________ TO __________
JOB TITLE ______________________________________
SALARY __________ REASON FOR LEAVING ______________________

EMPLOYER'S NAME ______________________ PHONE (___) ____________
ADDRESS ______________________________________
EMPLOYED FROM __________ TO __________
JOB TITLE ______________________________________
SALARY __________ REASON FOR LEAVING ______________________

EMPLOYER'S NAME ______________________ PHONE (___) ____________
ADDRESS ______________________________________
EMPLOYED FROM __________ TO __________
JOB TITLE ______________________________________
SALARY __________ REASON FOR LEAVING ______________________

EMPLOYER'S NAME ______________________ PHONE (___) ____________
ADDRESS ______________________________________
EMPLOYED FROM __________ TO __________
JOB TITLE ______________________________________
SALARY __________ REASON FOR LEAVING ______________________

EMPLOYMENT INFORMATION CONTINUED

NOTE: IT IS NOT NECESSARY TO USE THIS PAGE IF THE PREVIOUS PAGE CONTAINS SUFFICIENT SPACE FOR YOU TO PROVIDE THE INFORMATION WHICH HAD BEEN REQUESTED.

EMPLOYER'S NAME ______________________________ PHONE (___) __________
ADDRESS ______________________________
EMPLOYED FROM ________ TO ________
JOB TITLE ______________________________
SALARY __________ REASON FOR LEAVING ______________________________

EMPLOYER'S NAME ______________________________ PHONE (___) __________
ADDRESS ______________________________
EMPLOYED FROM ________ TO ________
JOB TITLE ______________________________
SALARY __________ REASON FOR LEAVING ______________________________

EMPLOYER'S NAME ______________________________ PHONE (___) __________
ADDRESS ______________________________
EMPLOYED FROM ________ TO ________
JOB TITLE ______________________________
SALARY __________ REASON FOR LEAVING ______________________________

EMPLOYER'S NAME ______________________________ PHONE (___) __________
ADDRESS ______________________________
EMPLOYED FROM ________ TO ________
JOB TITLE ______________________________
SALARY __________ REASON FOR LEAVING ______________________________

EMPLOYER'S NAME ______________________________ PHONE (___) __________
ADDRESS ______________________________
EMPLOYED FROM ________ TO ________
JOB TITLE ______________________________
SALARY __________ REASON FOR LEAVING ______________________________

EMPLOYER'S NAME ______________________________ PHONE (___) __________
ADDRESS ______________________________
EMPLOYED FROM ________ TO ________
JOB TITLE ______________________________
SALARY __________ REASON FOR LEAVING ______________________________

HAVE YOU EVER BEEN DISCHARGED OR ASKED TO RESIGN BY ANY OF YOUR PREVIOUS EMPLOYERS? ( ) YES ( ) NO IF YES, EXPLAIN.

____

____

____

SECTION VII - REFERENCES

LIST FIVE (5) REFERENCES, OTHER THAN RELATIVES, EMPLOYERS OR MEMBERS OF THIS DEPARTMENT, WHO KNOW YOU WELL ENOUGH TO GIVE INFORMATION ABOUT YOU.

NAME______________________________
ADDRESS______________________________ HOME PHONE (   )
______________ BUSINESS PHONE (   ) ______________
OCCUPATION ______________________ YEARS KNOWN __________

NAME______________________________
ADDRESS______________________________ HOME PHONE (   )
______________ BUSINESS PHONE (   ) ______________
OCCUPATION ______________________ YEARS KNOWN __________

NAME______________________________
ADDRESS______________________________ HOME PHONE (   )
______________ BUSINESS PHONE (   ) ______________
OCCUPATION ______________________ YEARS KNOWN __________

NAME______________________________
ADDRESS______________________________ HOME PHONE (   )
______________ BUSINESS PHONE (   ) ______________
OCCUPATION ______________________ YEARS KNOWN __________

NAME______________________________
ADDRESS______________________________ HOME PHONE (   )
______________ BUSINESS PHONE (   ) ______________
OCCUPATION ______________________ YEARS KNOWN __________

LIST MEMBERS OF LAW ENFORCEMENT AGENCIES YOU ARE ACQUAINTED WITH, TYPE OF RELATIONSHIP (RELATIVE, CLOSE FRIEND, NEIGHBOR, CASUAL ACQUAINTANCE, CO-WORKER, ETC.) AND THE NUMBER OF YEARS YOU HAVE KNOWN THEM.

NAME__________ YEARS KNOWN______ RELATIONSHIP ____
__________ ADDRESS__________
__________ HOME PHONE ( )__________
AGENCY __________

NAME__________ YEARS KNOWN______ RELATIONSHIP ____
__________ ADDRESS__________
__________ HOME PHONE ( )__________
AGENCY __________

NAME__________ YEARS KNOWN______ RELATIONSHIP ____
__________ ADDRESS__________
__________ HOME PHONE ( )__________
AGENCY __________

NAME__________ YEARS KNOWN______ RELATIONSHIP ____
__________ ADDRESS__________
__________ HOME PHONE ( )__________
AGENCY __________

NAME__________ YEARS KNOWN______ RELATIONSHIP ____
__________ ADDRESS__________
__________ HOME PHONE ( )__________
AGENCY __________

NAME__________ YEARS KNOWN______ RELATIONSHIP ____
__________ ADDRESS__________
__________ HOME PHONE ( )__________
AGENCY __________

SECTION VIII - ARREST INFORMATION

HAVE YOU EVER BEEN DETAINED FOR INVESTIGATION, QUESTIONED, HELD ON SUSPICION, FINGERPRINTED OR ARRESTED BY ANY LAW ENFORCEMENT AGENCY OR MILITARY AUTHORITY?

( ) YES ( ) NO

HAVE YOU EVER BEEN ARRESTED FOR A TRAFFIC VIOLATION? ( ) YES ( ) NO

WHILE IN THE MILITARY SERVICE, WHERE YOU EVER THE SUBJECT OF ANY DISCIPLINARY ACTION SUCH AS: COURTS MARTIAL, CAPTAIN'S MAST, OFFICE HOURS, COMPANY PUNISHMENT OR OTHERS?

( ) YES ( ) NO

IF THE ANSWER TO ANY OF THE ABOVE QUESTIONS IS YES, LIST THE INFORMATION BELOW AND WRITE A SHORT NARRATIVE ACCOUNT OF EACH INCIDENT.

DATE	CHARGE	AGENCY	PENALTY

HAVE YOU EVER BEEN REFUSED AN OPERATOR'S LICENSE BY ANY STATE? ( ) YES ( ) NO

IF THE ANSWER IS YES, GIVE THE DETAILS BELOW.

SECTION IX - TRAFFIC INFORMATION

LIST EVERY MOTOR VEHICLE OPERATOR'S LICENSE YOU HAVE POSSESSED.

STATE	NUMBER	APPROX. DATE OF ISSUE

LIST EVERY CITATION YOU HAVE RECEIVED FOR A MOVING OR EQUIPMENT VIOLATION.

DATE	CHARGE	DEPARTMENT OR AGENCY	PENALTY

HAS YOUR DRIVER'S LICENSE EVER BEEN SUSPENDED OR REVOKED OR HAVE YOU EVER RECEIVED A WARNING NOTICE FROM THE STATE THAT ISSUED YOUR LICENSE RELATED TO POSSIBLE SUSPENSION? (   ) YES (   ) NO

IF YES EXPLAIN BELOW.

HAVE YOU EVER BEEN INVOLVED IN A TRAFFIC ACCIDENT? (   ) YES (   )NO IF YES, DESCRIBE EACH ACCIDENT IN A BRIEF NARRATIVE INCLUDING DATE AND LOCATION.

SECTION X - EDUCATION INFORMATION

LIST EACH HIGH SCHOOL YOU HAVE ATTENDED. (START WITH LAST ONE ATTENDED.)

NAME OF SCHOOL	CITY & STATE	ATTENDANCE DATES	GRAD?	MAJOR
		FROM______TO_____		
		FROM______TO_____		
		FROM______TO_____		

LIST EACH COLLEGE/UNIVERSITY YOU HAVE ATTENDED.

NAME OF SCHOOL	CITY & STATE	ATTENDANCE DATES	GRAD?	MAJOR
		FROM______TO_____		
		FROM______TO_____		
		FROM______TO_____		

LIST ANY BUSINESS OR TRADE SCHOOLS YOU HAVE ATTENDED.

NAME OF SCHOOL	CITY & STATE	ATTENDANCE DATES	GRAD?	MAJOR
		FROM______TO_____		
		FROM______TO_____		
		FROM______TO_____		

IF YOU HAVE OBTAINED A G.E.D. (GENERAL EDUCATION DEVELOPMENT) HIGH SCHOOL LEVEL EQUIVALENT, PROVIDE THE FOLLOWING:

WHERE TAKEN ______________________________ WHEN ______________

LIST ANY CERTIFICATES OR LICENSES OF PROFESSIONAL OR VOCATIONAL COMPETENCE.

HAVE YOU EVER BEEN EXPELLED FROM ANY SCHOOL? (   ) YES (   ) NO IF YES, EXPLAIN.

LIST ANY COURSES/TRAINING YOU FEEL HAS A BEARING ON YOUR QUALIFICATIONS.

1.	2.
3.	4.
5.	6.

SECTION XI - MILITARY INFORMATION

LIST ALL ENLISTMENTS IN THE ARMED FORCES OF THE UNITED STATES.

ENLISTMENT DATE ____________ DISCHARGE DATE ____________ SERIAL NO. ____________

BRANCH OF SERVICE ________________________ UNIT ________________________

HIGHEST RANK ATTAINED ____

RANK/RATE AT DISCHARGE ____________________ TYPE OF DISCHARGE ____________

ENLISTMENT DATE ____________ DISCHARGE DATE ____________ SERIAL NO. ____________

BRANCH OF SERVICE ________________________ UNIT ________________________

HIGHEST RANK ATTAINED ________________________

RANK/RATE AT DISCHARGE ________________________

TYPE OF DISCHARGE ________________________

IF YOU RECEIVED A DISCHARGE OTHER THAN HONORABLE, EXPLAIN REASONS BELOW.

____

____

____

HAVE YOU SERVED IN THE ARMED FORCES OF ANY NATION OTHER THAN THE UNITED STATES?
( ) YES ( ) NO IF YES, LIST NATION(S), BRANCH OF SERVICE, DATE OF SERVICE AND RATE/RANK AT TIME OF DISCHARGE.

____

____

LIST YOUR MILITARY RESERVE STATUS: ( ) ACTIVE ( ) INACTIVE ( ) NONE
BRANCH OF SERVICE ________________________ UNIT ____________
UNIT ADDRESS ____
DATE OF ENLISTMENT ____________ END OF ENLISTMENT ____________ RATE/RANK ________
COMMANDING OFFICER ________________________

LIST YOUR MILITARY RESERVE OBLIGATIONS.

____

____

____

____

____

SECTION XIII - ORGANIZATION INFORMATION

LIST JOB RELATED PROFESSIONAL SOCIETIES/ORGANIZATIONS TO WHICH YOU NOW OR HAVE BELONGED.

ORGANIZATION ____________________

ADDRESS ____________________

MEMBER FROM ________ TO ________ OFFICE HELD ____________________

ORGANIZATION ____________________

ADDRESS ____________________

MEMBER FROM ________ TO ________ OFFICE HELD ____________________

ORGANIZATION ____________________

ADDRESS ____________________

MEMBER FROM ________ TO ________ OFFICE HELD ____________________

ORGANIZATION ____________________

ADDRESS ____________________

MEMBER FROM ________ TO ________ OFFICE HELD ____________________

SECTION XIV - MISCELLANEOUS INFORMATION

LIST ANY SPECIAL AWARDS YOU HAVE RECEIVED, HONORS THAT MAY HAVE BEEN BESTOWED UPON YOU, OR QUALIFICATIONS YOU MAY POSSESS WHICH HAVE NOT BEEN MENTIONED.

HAVE YOU EVER FILED FOR AN EXAMINATION WITH THIS DEPARTMENT OR ANY OTHER POLICE AGENCY?
( ) YES ( ) NO

DATE	FILED	DEPARTMENT OR AGENCY RESULTS

DESCRIBE IN YOUR OWN WORDS YOUR USE OF INTOXICATING BEVERAGES.

DO YOU NOW, OR HAVE YOU EVER USED ANY NARCOTICS AND/OR DANGEROUS DRUGS?
( ) YES ( ) NO IF YOU CHECKED "YES," PLEASE EXPLAIN BELOW:

IF IT BECAME NECESSARY IN THE COURSE OF YOUR POLICE DUTIES TO TAKE A HUMAN LIFE, WOULD YOU HAVE ANY RELUCTANCE TO DO SO BECAUSE OF RELIGIOUS OR OTHER REASONS?
( ) YES ( ) NO ( ) N/A/ IF "YES," PLEASE EXPLAIN:

PAGE NO.	IDENTIFY EACH ITEM BY PAGE NUMBER AND TITLE OR TYPE OF ITEM WHICH IS BEING EXPLAINED.

I AM AWARE THAT ANY MISREPRESENTATIONS OR FALSIFICATIONS MADE IN CONNECTION WITH MY OBTAINING EMPLOYMENT WITH THE LATAH COUNTY SHERIFF'S OFFICE WILL BE GROUNDS FOR REJECTION OR DISMISSAL.

DATE _______________ SIGNATURE ____

Chapter Nine
The Training Academy

Police training facilities are designed to prepare newly hired law enforcement employees, as well as prospective applicants, for the job. Most of the training facilities are run in a manner similar to paramilitary training.

Paramilitary means after a military pattern. Although the command structures of law enforcement academies are basically paramilitary, over the years the physical and mental stress associated with these types of training facilities have dictated a move away from the *Boot Camp* style of training toward spending more time in the classrooms and practical training situations.

The length of a training academy's session varies from agency to agency. Usually it is a minimum of ten weeks in length, but it can last as long as five months. The length of time you spend at the academy will depend upon the agency for which you work.

There are stringent physical fitness requirements, and the responsibility of maintaining them falls on the recruit. In other words, you will have to train yourself to prepare for the physical fitness requirements during your free time. It is not part of the regular training schedule.

Although there will be physical fitness training and workouts as a part of the academy's program, the time dedicated to these activities is not likely to be adequate to prepare a recruit to be able to pass the physical agility testing unless he or she is already in first-class shape. The Academy's testing is similar to the physical agility test described in Chapter Four.

If you feel you are going to need additional physical fitness training, consider having a trainer at a local gym set up a weight training program for you prior to entering the academy. Then stick with this program throughout your stay at the academy. Because most academies have two or three physical fitness tests during a session, do not give up if you fail the first test. Use it to identify your weaknesses and work toward strengthening them in the time that remains.

Each training academy's sessions concentrate on the different aspects of the law that pertain to that particular field. For example, the FBI Academy instructs its students on federal laws. Although they will also teach many other types of law enforcement procedures, state laws, and civil laws, their concentration will be on federal law because the job of the FBI is to enforce federal laws.

State Patrol and Highway Patrol Academies spend a great deal of time teaching traffic laws and traffic accident investigation. The task of local Police and Sheriff's Academies is more difficult. They must teach a little bit of everything. This is not an indication that these academies are more difficult to complete, but they simply have to cover the fact that a local police officer or sheriff's deputy must deal with problems that arise in all types of legal areas — municipal laws, civil laws, city ordinances, federal laws, traffic laws, penal codes, health and welfare codes, alcoholic beverage laws, etc.

A law teacher's comment to a class of new recruits sums it all up. "I have four months to cram four years of law school into your brains."

In general, most training academies teach a specific area of law enforcement to their students. However, they also teach arrest techniques, self defense including hand-to-hand combat, use of a baton and chemical agents such as mace, and firearms qualification with a handgun, shotgun, high-powered rifle, and possibly automatic weapons.

In addition, they teach defensive driving, pursuit driving techniques, crime scene investigation, evidence collection, and radio procedures. There are also classes in effective written communication that include report writing, spelling, and punctuation.

Although it may be hard work, the session at the police or training academy of your chosen law enforcement agency will be an exciting and rewarding accomplishment. A word of warning, however, do not give up or show signs of defeat to an instructor.

If you are injured or unable to complete the academy for some other reason such as your academic performance, ask a class counselor to help you prepare for the next class. You will find they are very supportive and will help you in any way they can. You would probably be surprised to learn how many law enforcement professionals attended the academy more than once before they successfully graduated.

Police officers never give up because if they do, it may very well cost them their lives.

Life at the Training Academy

New recruits arrive for the Training Academy session

Recruits being instructed to empty suitcases on the ground for inspection

New recruit being read off by training academy instructor

Recruits filling out the necessary forms for the Academy

Classroom participation at the Training Academy

Academy class being instructed in knowledge of the laws for their particular jurisdiction

Recruits marching from the classroom

Academy trainee writing a report

Practicing defensive driving and pursuit driving on the Academy driving course

Academy trainees learning self-defense techniques

© 1996 Mark C. Ide

Even mealtimes are used for study at the Academy

Photograph courtesy of Robert J. Piel

The big day arrives — graduation at last!

Chapter Ten
Questions & Answers

Introduction

The following questions are ones that many people wonder about when considering a position in law enforcement. The answers are of a general nature because some agencies may have specialized situations in which the specific requirements differ from those that apply generally. However, these answers will apply to almost all agencies.

General Questions

Am I too old?

Most agencies have raised or abolished their age requirements in recent years. If you appear to be in good physical health and are under the age of fifty, you should not have a problem.

Will I be able to negotiate my salary?

Unless you have prior experience in law enforcement, you will not be able to negotiate your salary. If you do have prior experience in law enforcement, make sure your experience is an obvious asset to the agency.

How long will it be before I am hired?

In most cases, the hiring process will take from three to six months. However, depending on the size of the agency, it could take up to a year. Just be patient and do not give up. You will eventually be hired.

Can I appeal or contest the results of a particular test if I should fail to pass it?

If you have a good reason, most agencies will hear your complaint. If you are convincing, they will allow you to take that particular test again. Illness, family emergencies, and injury are commonly accepted reasons for retesting.

Should I apply to more than one agency at a time?

Yes! We strongly recommend that you apply to several agencies at the same time. It is like playing the lottery. The more tickets you purchase, the better your chances are of winning.

What are the training academies like?

Although the requirements vary from one jurisdiction to another, it is similar to a military boot camp. Your stay there will range from four weeks to six months, depending on your requirements.

Personal Questions

What will happen if I have a prior arrest as a juvenile?

Depending on the crime, your criminal history record as a juvenile will be closed. If you do have an arrest record, we suggest you do not try to hide it. A background investigator will more than likely discover the arrest and decide you are trying to hide it from them. This, of course, will disqualify you from consideration.

Will a traffic ticket for speeding disqualify me?

In most cases, if you have more than two traffic tickets for a moving violation (other than parking tickets), you will have to do a lot of explaining. Having several traffic tickets shows an unwillingness to obey the laws.

I have not completed High School. Will this disqualify me?

Yes, You must have graduated from high school or possess a GED equivalency certificate.

I was arrested for a misdemeanor but never convicted of a crime. Will this hurt my chances of getting hired?

Depending on the situation, it may. A background investigator will check into the arrest thoroughly and make a determination from his findings. Again, be honest from the beginning and try not to hide anything.

Are there any classes I can take that will help me get hired?

Yes. Most Community Colleges have courses in criminal justice. These courses range from the laws of arrest to collection of evidence. Taking these courses will show an interest in and a willingness to become a law enforcement officer.

Drug Usage

I have used marijuana on a few occasions, but only recreationally. Will this hurt my chances of getting hired?

It may, but it will depend on your age when you last ingested marijuana and how many years ago it was. Most people have experimented as a juvenile. However, if you have used marijuana in the last year, you are better off waiting for one year before applying.

While I was at a party, someone had Cocaine and I tried it. Will this disqualify me from being hired?

As with Marijuana and all other illegal narcotics, it may disqualify you. Unfortuately in our society today, some drugs are becoming acceptable. How long ago you tried the drug will have a major effect. Again, if you have used any illegal narcotic in the last year, you are better off waiting for a year before applying. Then you must have a very good explanation for the reason you used the drug.

If I admit to having used drugs in the past can I be arrested?

No. The use of most illegal narcotics is a misdemeanor, and you can only be arrested if it was committed in the presence of a police officer.

These questions and their responses should answer most of the questions you have about applying for a position with a law enforcement agency.

Conclusion

The authors who have a combined twenty-five years of experience in law enforcement have found it to be a very rewarding career. Like a career in any other profession, there are times its downside seems to prevail — a case that is difficult to solve, a dangerous suspect, a conviction that is overturned, fatigue from long hours on the job, or seeing lives snuffed out in a senseless accident. However, the rewards that prevail over the disheartening events that often occur far surpass anything that can happen on the downside. Such things as reviving a lifeless baby who was found floating in a pool of water, removing injured people from a burning building, or even less notable acts such as just talking with a person on the street who needs someone to talk to help us to feel that we are of service to our fellow mankind and our lives are being lived in a worthwhile manner.

Looking back to the years of my childhood, I can remember reading a story about a local police officer who found himself dealing with a difficult theft case. While on patrol, he come across a mentally retarded man who had been accosted by members of a local street gang. During the attack they took his radio. The officer, knowing that the case would never be solved, did what any true police officer would do, he drove the victim to a store and purchased him a new radio.

That single incident affected two people for the rest of their lives. It restored the happiness of a disabled victim, and created another dedicated police officer to protect the rights of the citizens of this country. The new officer was me, and that compassionate police officer from many years ago was my brother, Kennth R. Piel.

Paul van der Linden and I hope this book will encourage persons of the greatest character and compassion to step forward and protect the citizens of our country. We would encourage you to continue your pursuit of a career in law enforcement by following the guidelines contained in this book.

The best of luck to you!

Robert J. Piel
Officer, Federal Way, Washington Police Department

Paul C. Van Der Linden
Officer, Irwindale, California Police Department, Retired

Appendix A — Answer Key

The following pages contain the answers to the True/False Questions found at the end of each chapter.

Chapter One
The Application

Page 1-16

1. F (Page 1-3)
2. T (Page 1-3)
3. F (Page 1-3)
4. F (Page 1-6)
5. T (Page 1-10)
6. F (Page 1-4)
7. T (Page 1-7)
8. T (Page 1-4)
9. T (Page 1-9)
10. F (Pages 1-7, 1-10)

Chapter Two
The Written Exam

Page 2-14

1. T (Page 2-3)
2. T (Page 2-3)
3. F (Page 1-3)
4. T (Page 2-5)
5. F (Page 2-5)
6. T (Page 2-5)
7. T (Page 2-4)
8. F (Page 2-7)
9. F (Page 2-7)
10. F (Page 2-9)

Chapter Three
The Physical Agility Test

Page 3-9

1. F (Page 3-8)
2. T (Page 3-3)
3. F (Pages 3-3, 3-8)
4. F (Page 3-3)
5. T (Page 3-8)
6. T (Page 3-2)
7. T (Page 3-3)
8. F (Page 3-8)
9. T (Page 3-3)
10. T (Page 3-8)

Chapter Four
The Oral Interview

Page 4-18, 4-19

1. T (Page 4-2)
2. T (Page 4-4)
3. F (Page 4-4)
4. F (Page 4-5)
5. T (Page 4-5)
6. F (Page 4-5)
7. T (Pages 4-6, 4-16)
8. T (Page 4-7)
9. F (Page 4-6)
10. T (Page 4-4)

Index